Am
Minor

Chord Spelling

1st (A), ♭3rd (C), 5th (E)

Left hand suggestion: 1st (root note) and 5th

FREE ACCESS on smartphones including iPhone & Android

Using any free QR code app, scan and **HEAR** the chord

A+
Augmented Triad

Chord Spelling

1st (A), 3rd (C♯), ♯5th (E♯)

Left hand suggestion: 1st (root note) and 5th

FREE ACCESS on smartphones
including iPhone & Android

Using any free QR code app,
scan and **HEAR** the chord

Easy to Use
PICK UP & PLAY
PIANO CHORDS
SEE IT HEAR IT
JAKE JACKSON
Flame Tree Music
mobile
online
in print
Flame Tree Music
BOOKS · eBOOKS · RESOURCES

Contents

Publisher/Creative Director: Nick Wells • Project, design and media integration: Jake Jackson • Website and software: David Neville with Stevens Dumpala and Steve Moulton • Editorial: Laura Bulbeck

First published 2016 by **FLAME TREE PUBLISHING**
6 Melbray Mews, Fulham, London SW6 3NS, United Kingdom
www.flametreepublishing.com

Music information site: www.flametreemusic.com

18 19 20 21 22 • 4 5 6 7 8 9 10

The CIP record for this book is available from the British Library.

ISBN: 978-1-78361-921-4

Jake Jackson is a writer and musician. He has created and contributed to over 25 practical music books, including *Reading Music Made Easy*, *Play Flamenco* and *Piano and Keyboard Chords*. His music is available on iTunes, Amazon and Spotify amongst others.

Piano Chords
An Introduction

Chord books for piano and keyboard players are essential for anyone who wants to play in a band with other musicians, or quickly work out the structure of a popular song. As a songwriting tool, they're an absolute must. Thank you for choosing ours, we created it with *you* in mind!

We've tried to make this book as straightforward as possible, without compromising its useability, so:

1. You can quickly find your way to the chord you want, work out what to play, and, **hear the chord online**.

2. The chord selection focuses on those most commonly used. It's these chords that form the basis of the songs you hear on the radio, online and in stores. Most of the popular **rock, pop, blues, folk** and **country** tunes use only four or five chords in total.

3. A few interesting chords have been added for experimentation, and to offer you an insight into other chord forms which will help you extend your musical vocabulary.

4. All chords are in the first position only, to allow us to provide a wide enough selection. Our website (**flametreemusic.com**) shows the second position too, and you can **hear** them there too.

5. Keep the book at home or in a bag, it's a great long term resource.

Playing the guitar, in a band, on your own, writing for others, or just playing along to your headphones, **Pick up and Play Piano Chords** will help you get the most out of your guitar. Enjoy it!

Chord Diagrams
A Quick Guide

The chord diagrams are designed for quick access. You can flick through the book using the tabs on the side, then copy the finger positions and keyboard to help you make the chord.

- Each chord is provided with a **Chord Spelling** to help you check the notes. This is a great way to learn the structure of the sounds you are making and will help with harmonies.

- The chords in this book are for the **right hand only**, so we can fit in as many as possible. Generally they should be played to the right of middle C, and where necessary we indicate where middle C falls in relation to the chord played.

- To play the **bass notes** on the **left hand** it is best to start by using the **root note** (the **1st note** of the name) of the chord, and perhaps the 5th note, to give power to the sound. The root note can be an **octave lower** (or two) than the same note on the right hand.

- For more **complex chords** we assume you will play the root note with the left hand, and the other notes on the right.

Each page reminds you how to use the left hand

FREE ACCESS on smartphones including iPhone & Android

Using any free QR code app, scan and **HEAR** the chord

The Basics

Chord name: Each chord is given a short and complete name, so the short name C°7 is properly known as C Diminished 7th.

Right Hand Fingerings:

- **1** is the thumb
- **2** is the index finger
- **3** is the middle finger
- **4** is the ring finger
- **5** is the little finger

Names of the black notes on the keyboard

Chord name

Tabs help give quick access to the keys

Guide position of middle C

Starting note of the diagram

Names of the white notes on the keyboard

Right Hand Fingering

Notes of the Chord

Dm
Minor

C♯D♭ D♯E♭   F♯G♭ G♯A♭ A♯B♭

Middle C

1   **2**   **4**

C D E F G A B

Chord Spelling
1st (D), ♭3rd (F), 5th (A)
Left hand suggestion: 1st (root note) and 5th

FREE ACCESS on smartphones including iPhone & Android

Using any free QR code app, scan and **HEAR** the chord

FREE ACCESS on smartphones including iPhone & Android

Using any free QR code app, scan and **HEAR** the chord

The Sound Links
Another Quick Guide

Requirements: a camera and internet ready smartphone (eg. **iPhone**, any **Android** phone (e.g. **Samsung Galaxy**), **Nokia Lumia**, or **camera-enabled tablet** such as the **iPad Mini**). The best result is achieved using a WIFI connection.

1. Download any **free QR code reader**. An app store search will reveal a great many of these, so obviously its is best to go with the ones with the highest ratings and don't be afraid to try a few before you settle on the one that works best for you. Tapmedia's QR Reader app is good, or ATT Scanner (used below) or QR Media. Some of the free apps have ads, which can be annoying.

2. Find the chord you want to play, look at the diagram then check out the **QR code** at the base of the page.

FREE ACCESS on smartphones including iPhone & Android

Using any free QR code app, scan and **HEAR** the chord

78

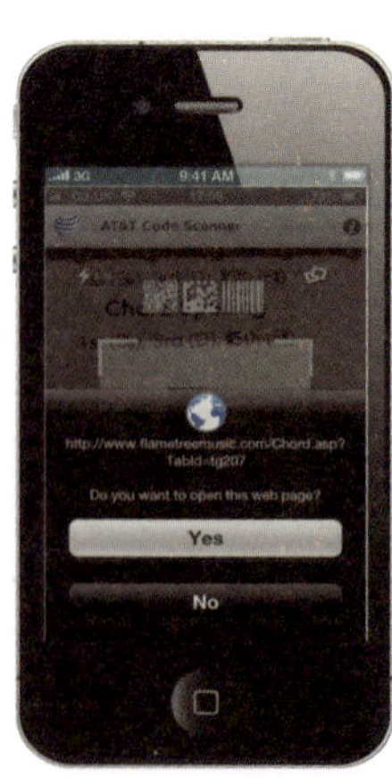

3. On your smartphone, open the app and **scan** the **QR code** at the base of any particular chord page.

4. The QR reader app will take you to a browser, then the specific chord will be displayed on the flame-treemusic.com website.

FREE ACCESS on smartphones including iPhone & Android

Using any free QR code app, scan and **HEAR** the chord

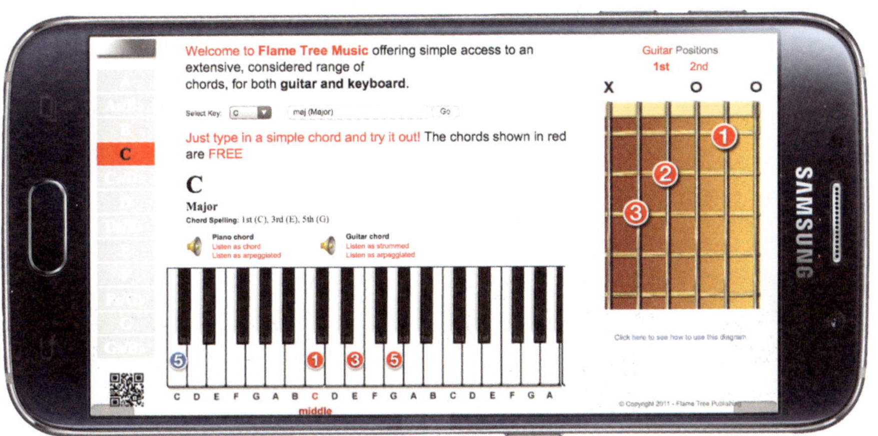

5. Using the usual pinch and zoom techniques, you can focus on four sound options.

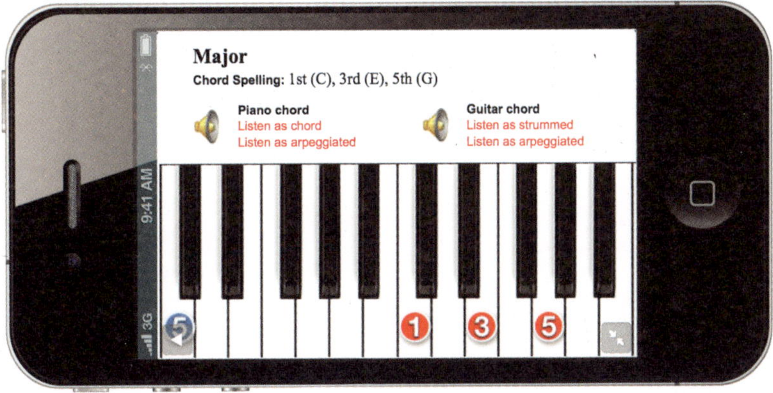

6. Click the sounds! Both piano and guitar audio is provided. This is particularly helpful when you're playing with others.

The QR codes give you direct access to all the chords. You can access a much wider range of chords if you register and subscribe.

FREE ACCESS on smartphones including iPhone & Android

Using any free QR code app, scan and **HEAR** the chord

A
Major

Chord Spelling

1st (A), 3rd (C♯), 5th (E)

Left hand suggestion: 1st (root note) and 5th

FREE ACCESS on smartphones including iPhone & Android

Using any free QR code app, scan and **HEAR** the chord

A°
Diminished Triad

Chord Spelling

1st (A), ♭3rd (C), ♭5th (E♭)

Left hand suggestion: 1st (root note) and 5th

FREE ACCESS on smartphones including iPhone & Android

Using any free QR code app, scan and **HEAR** the chord

Asus2
Suspended 2nd

Chord Spelling

1st (A), 2nd (B), 5th (E)

Left hand suggestion: 1st (root note) and 5th

FREE ACCESS on smartphones including iPhone & Android

Using any free QR code app, scan and **HEAR** the chord

Asus4
Suspended 4th

Chord Spelling

1st (A), 4th (D), 5th (E)

Left hand suggestion: 1st (root note) and 5th

FREE ACCESS on smartphones including iPhone & Android

Using any free QR code app, scan and **HEAR** the chord

A5
5th (Power Chord)

Chord Spelling

1st (A), 5th (E)

Left hand suggestion: 1st (root note) and 5th

FREE ACCESS on smartphones including iPhone & Android

Using any free QR code app, scan and **HEAR** the chord

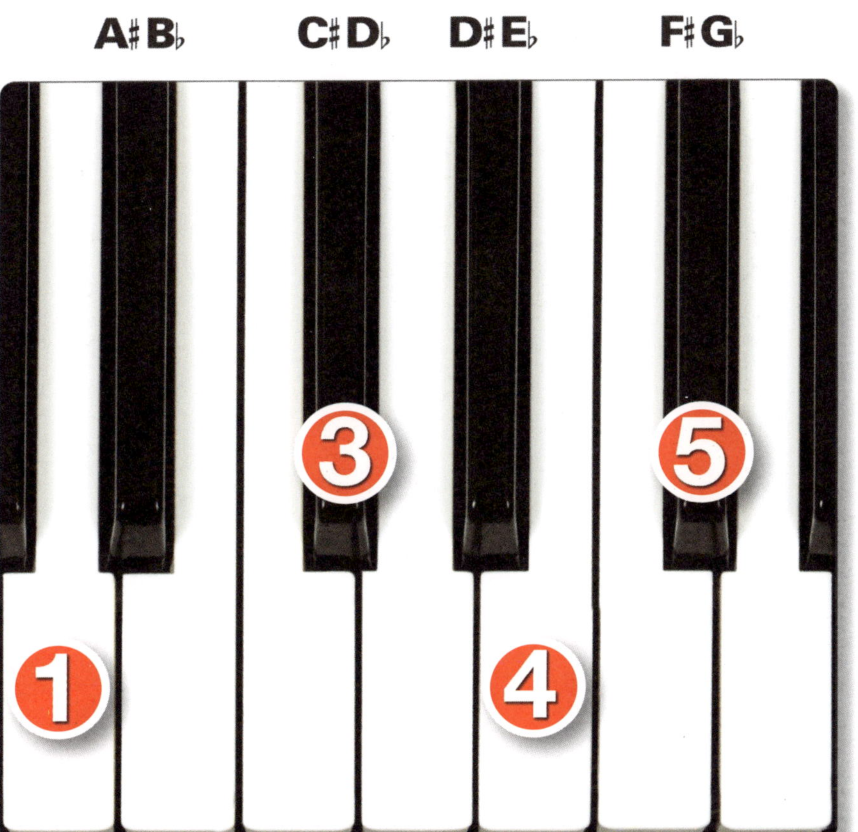

A6
Major 6th

Chord Spelling

1st (A), 3rd (C♯), 5th (E), 6th (F♯)

Left hand suggestion: 1st (root note) and 5th

FREE ACCESS on smartphones including iPhone & Android

Using any free QR code app, scan and **HEAR** the chord

Am6
Minor 6th

Chord Spelling

1st (A), ♭3rd (C), 5th (E), 6th (F♯)

Left hand suggestion: 1st (root note) and 5th

FREE ACCESS on smartphones including iPhone & Android

Using any free QR code app, scan and **HEAR** the chord

Amaj7
Major 7th

Chord Spelling

1st (A), 3rd (C#), 5th (E), 7th (G#)

Left hand suggestion: 1st (root note) and 5th

FREE ACCESS on smartphones
including iPhone & Android

Using any free QR code app,
scan and **HEAR** the chord

Am7
Minor 7th

Chord Spelling
1st (A), ♭3rd (C), 5th (E), ♭7th (G)

Left hand suggestion: 1st (root note) and 5th

FREE ACCESS on smartphones including iPhone & Android

Using any free QR code app, scan and **HEAR** the chord

A7
Dominant 7th

Chord Spelling

1st (A), 3rd (C♯), 5th (E), ♭7th (G)

Left hand suggestion: 1st (root note) and 5th

FREE ACCESS on smartphones
including iPhone & Android

Using any free QR code app,
scan and **HEAR** the chord

A°7
Diminished 7th

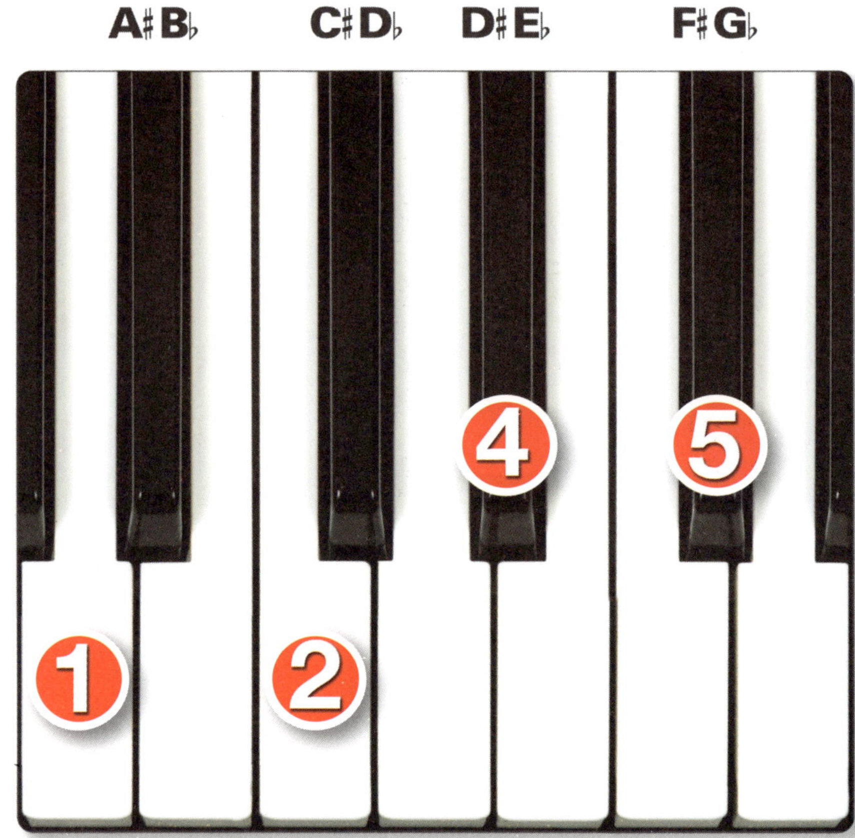

Chord Spelling

1st (A), ♭3rd (C), ♭5th (E♭), ♭♭7th (G♭)

Left hand suggestion: 1st (root note) and 5th

Amaj9
Major 9th

Chord Spelling

1st (A), 3rd (C#), 5th (E), 7th (G#), 9th (B)

Left hand suggestion: 1st (root note) and 5th

FREE ACCESS on smartphones including iPhone & Android

Using any free QR code app, scan and **HEAR** the chord

A♯/B♭
Major

Chord Spelling

1st (B♭), 3rd (D), 5th (F)

Left hand suggestion: 1st (root note) and 5th

FREE ACCESS on smartphones
including iPhone & Android

Using any free QR code app,
scan and **HEAR** the chord

A♯/B♭m
Minor

Chord Spelling

1st (B♭), ♭3rd (D♭), 5th (F)

Left hand suggestion: 1st (root note) and 5th

FREE ACCESS on smartphones including iPhone & Android

Using any free QR code app, scan and **HEAR** the chord

A♯/B♭+
Augmented Triad

Chord Spelling

1st (B♭), 3rd (D), ♯5th (F♯)

Left hand suggestion: 1st (root note) and 5th

FREE ACCESS on smartphones including iPhone & Android

Using any free QR code app, scan and **HEAR** the chord

A♯/B♭°
Diminished Triad

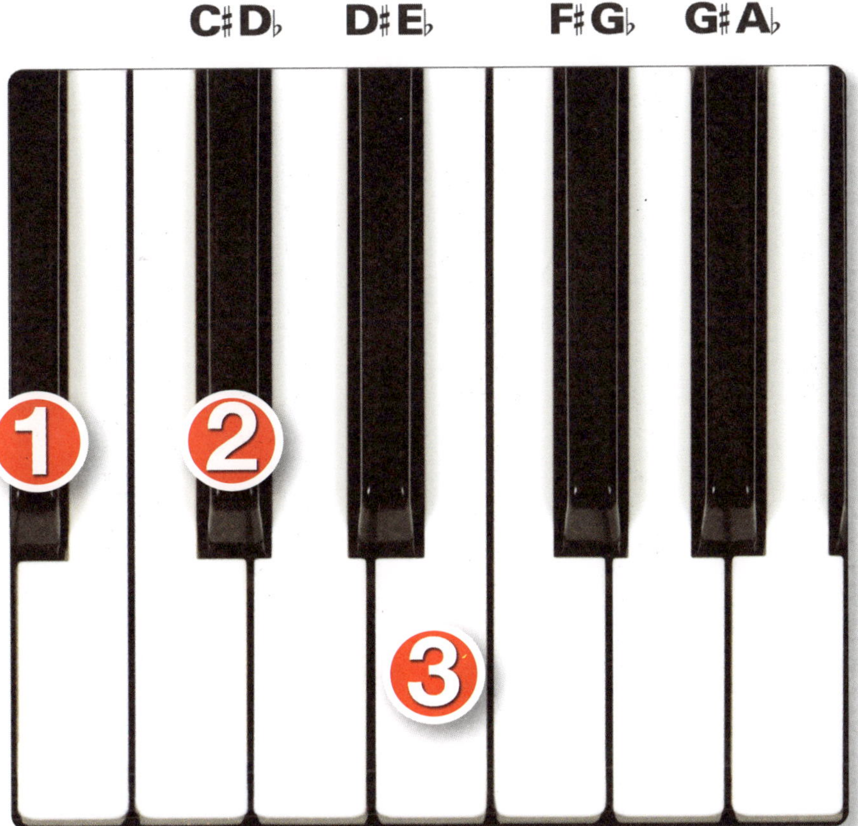

Chord Spelling

1st (B♭), ♭3rd (D♭), ♭5th (F♭)

Left hand suggestion: 1st (root note) and 5th

FREE ACCESS on smartphones including iPhone & Android

Using any free QR code app, scan and **HEAR** the chord

A♯/B♭sus2
Suspended 2nd

Chord Spelling

1st (B♭), 2nd (C), 5th (F)

Left hand suggestion: 1st (root note) and 5th

FREE ACCESS on smartphones
including iPhone & Android

Using any free QR code app,
scan and **HEAR** the chord

A♯/B♭sus4
Suspended 4th

Chord Spelling

1st (B♭), 4th (E♭), 5th (F)

Left hand suggestion: 1st (root note) and 5th

FREE ACCESS on smartphones including iPhone & Android

Using any free QR code app, scan and **HEAR** the chord

A♯/B♭5
5th (Power Chord)

Chord Spelling

1st (B♭), 5th (F)

Left hand suggestion: 1st (root note) and 5th

FREE ACCESS on smartphones including iPhone & Android

Using any free QR code app, scan and **HEAR** the chord

A♯/B♭6
Major 6th

Chord Spelling

1st (B♭), 3rd (D), 5th (F), 6th (G)

Left hand suggestion: 1st (root note) and 5th

FREE ACCESS on smartphones including iPhone & Android

Using any free QR code app, scan and **HEAR** the chord

A♯/B♭m6
Minor 6th

Chord Spelling

1st (B♭), ♭3rd (D♭), 5th (F), 6th (G)

Left hand suggestion: 1st (root note) and 5th

FREE ACCESS on smartphones
including iPhone & Android

Using any free QR code app,
scan and **HEAR** the chord

A♯/B♭maj7
Major 7th

C♯D♭   D♯E♭   F♯G♭   G♯A♭

B C D E F G A

Chord Spelling

1st (B♭), 3rd (D), 5th (F), 7th (A)

Left hand suggestion: 1st (root note) and 5th

FREE ACCESS on smartphones
including iPhone & Android

Using any free QR code app,
scan and **HEAR** the chord

A♯/B♭m7
Minor 7th

Chord Spelling

1st (B♭), ♭3rd (D♭), 5th (F), ♭7th (A♭)

Left hand suggestion: 1st (root note) and 5th

FREE ACCESS on smartphones
including iPhone & Android

Using any free QR code app,
scan and **HEAR** the chord

A♯/B♭7
Dominant 7th

Chord Spelling

1st (B♭), 3rd (D), 5th (F), ♭7th (A♭)

Left hand suggestion: 1st (root note) and 5th

FREE ACCESS on smartphones
including iPhone & Android

Using any free QR code app,
scan and **HEAR** the chord

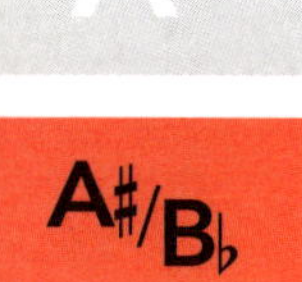

A♯/B♭°7
Diminished 7th

Chord Spelling

1st (B♭), ♭3rd (D♭), ♭5th (F♭), ♭♭7th (A♭♭)

Left hand suggestion: 1st (root note) and 5th

FREE ACCESS on smartphones
including iPhone & Android

Using any free QR code app,
scan and **HEAR** the chord

A♯/B♭maj9
Major 9th

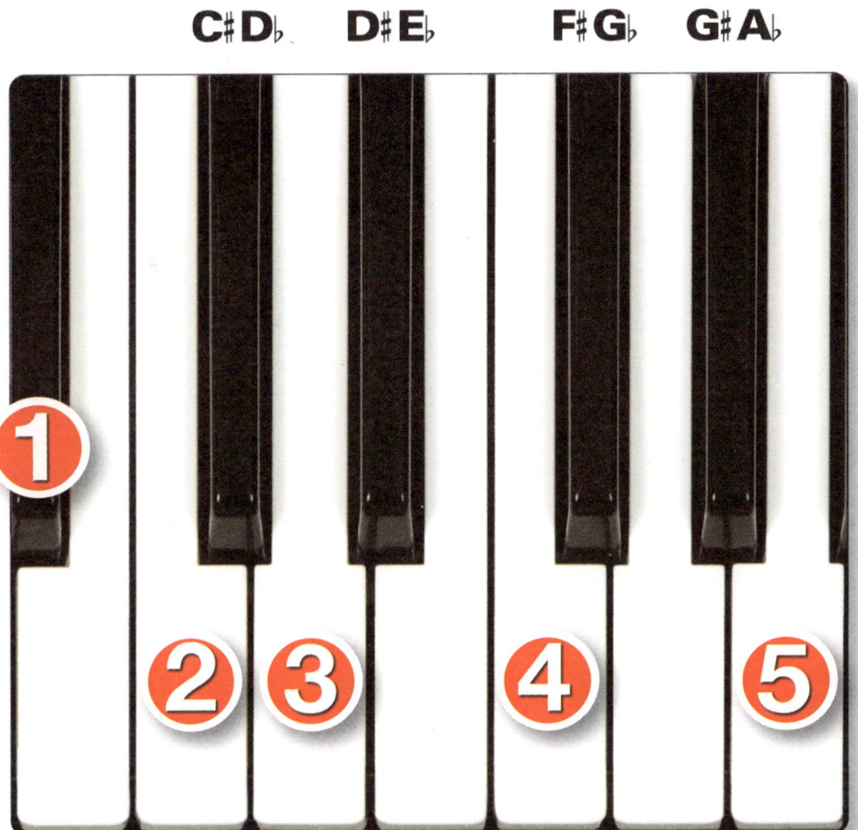

Chord Spelling

1st (B♭), 3rd (D), 5th (F), 7th (A), 9th (C)

Left hand suggestion: 1st (root note) and 5th

FREE ACCESS on smartphones
including iPhone & Android

Using any free QR code app,
scan and **HEAR** the chord

B
Major

Chord Spelling

1st (B), 3rd (D#), 5th (F#)

Left hand suggestion: 1st (root note) and 5th

FREE ACCESS on smartphones including iPhone & Android

Using any free QR code app, scan and **HEAR** the chord

Bm
Minor

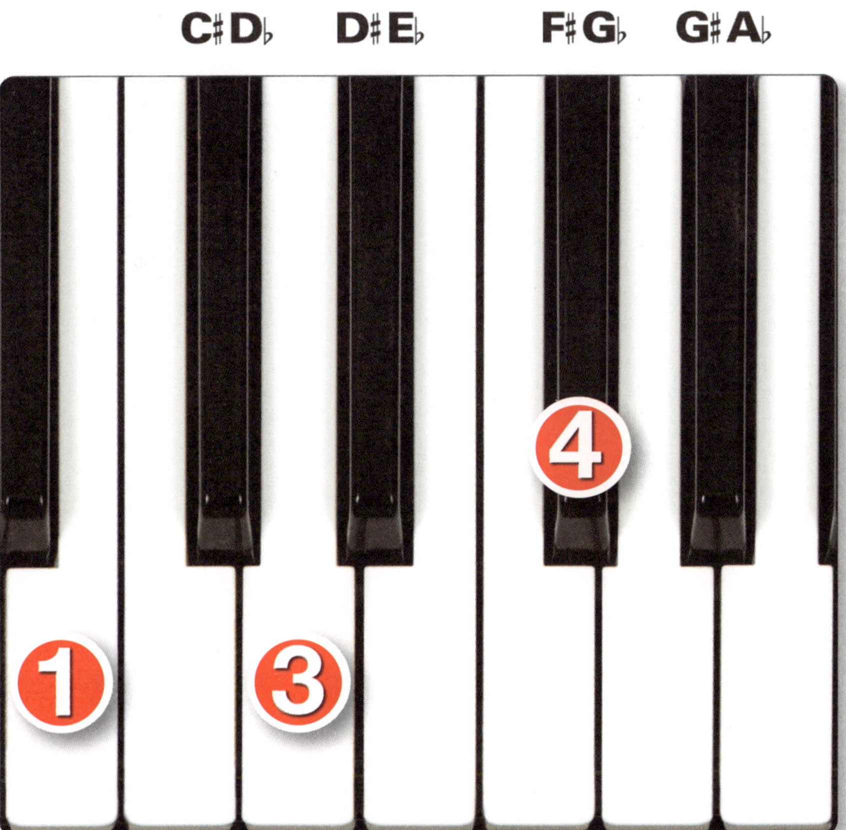

Chord Spelling

1st (B), ♭3rd (D), 5th (F♯)

Left hand suggestion: 1st (root note) and 5th

FREE ACCESS on smartphones including iPhone & Android

Using any free QR code app, scan and **HEAR** the chord

B+
Augmented Triad

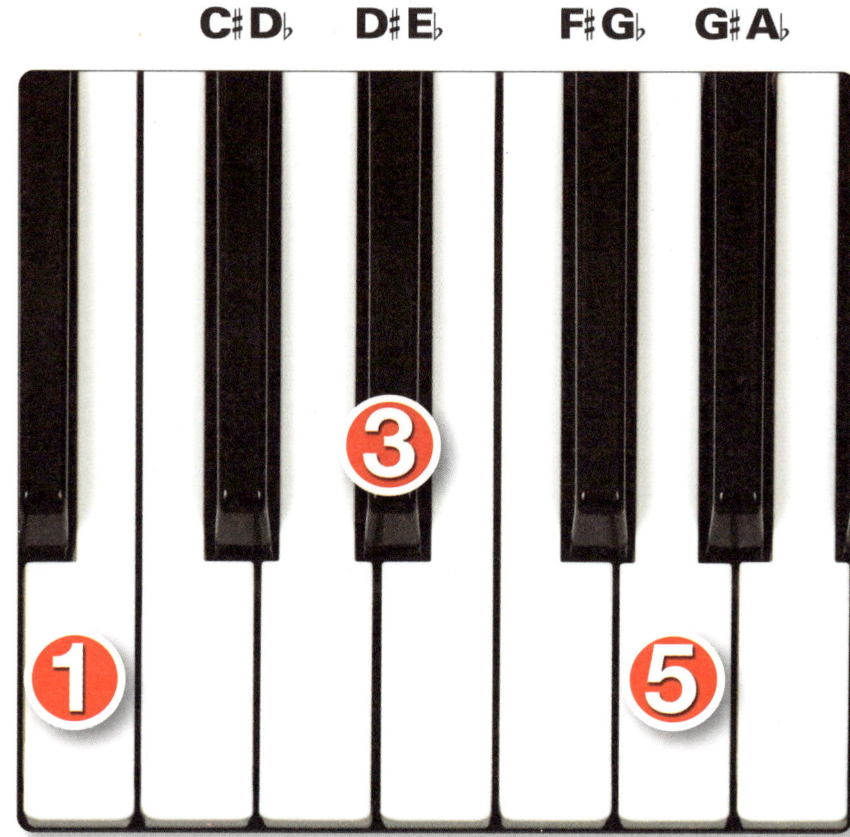

Chord Spelling
1st (B), 3rd (D♯), ♯5th (Fx)

Left hand suggestion: 1st (root note) and 5th

B°
Diminished Triad

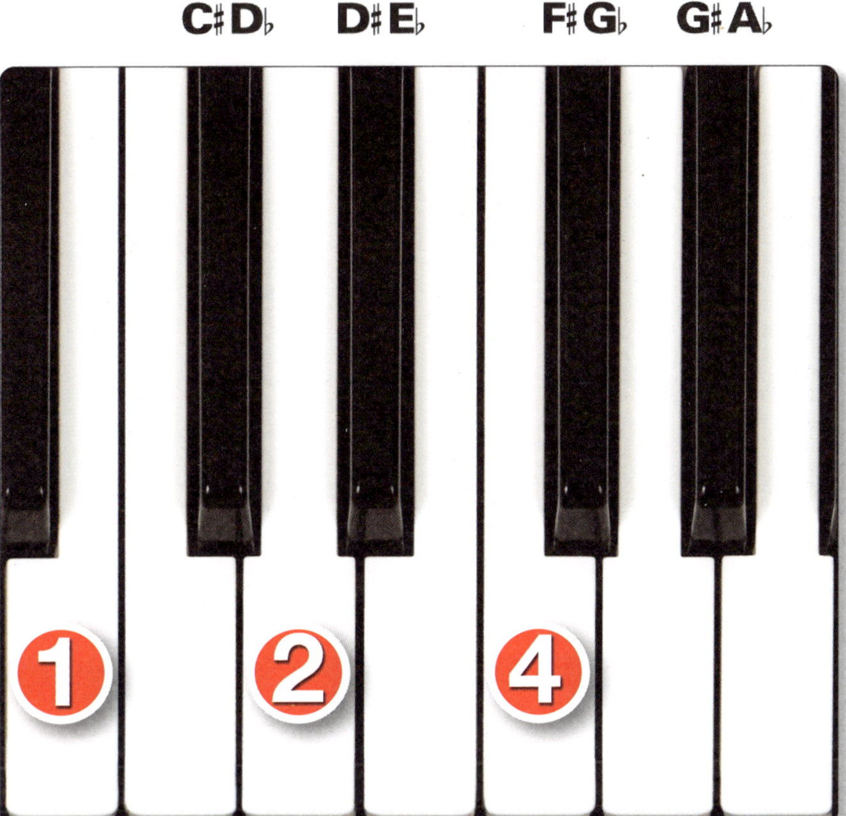

Chord Spelling

1st (B), ♭3rd (D), ♭5th (F)

Left hand suggestion: 1st (root note) and 5th

FREE ACCESS on smartphones including iPhone & Android

Using any free QR code app, scan and **HEAR** the chord

Bsus2
Suspended 2nd

Chord Spelling

1st (B), 2nd (C♯), 5th (F♯)

Left hand suggestion: 1st (root note) and 5th

FREE ACCESS on smartphones including iPhone & Android

Using any free QR code app, scan and **HEAR** the chord

Bsus4
Suspended 4th

Chord Spelling

1st (B), 4th (E), 5th (F♯)

Left hand suggestion: 1st (root note) and 5th

FREE ACCESS on smartphones including iPhone & Android

Using any free QR code app, scan and **HEAR** the chord

B5
5th (Power Chord)

Chord Spelling

1st (B), 5th (F♯)

Left hand suggestion: 1st (root note) and 5th

FREE ACCESS on smartphones including iPhone & Android

Using any free QR code app, scan and **HEAR** the chord

B6
Major 6th

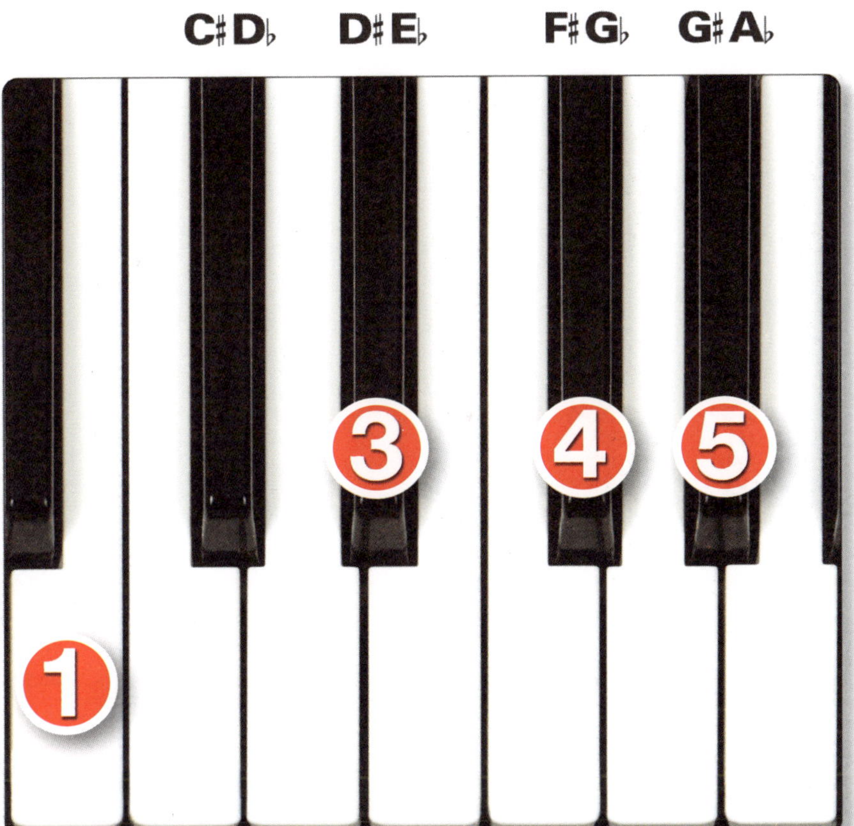

Chord Spelling

1st (B), 3rd (D♯), 5th (F♯), 6th (G♯)

Left hand suggestion: 1st (root note) and 5th

Bm6
Minor 6th

Chord Spelling

1st (B), ♭3rd (D), 5th (F#), 6th (G#)

Left hand suggestion: 1st (root note) and 5th

FREE ACCESS on smartphones
including iPhone & Android

Using any free QR code app,
scan and **HEAR** the chord

Bmaj7
Major 7th

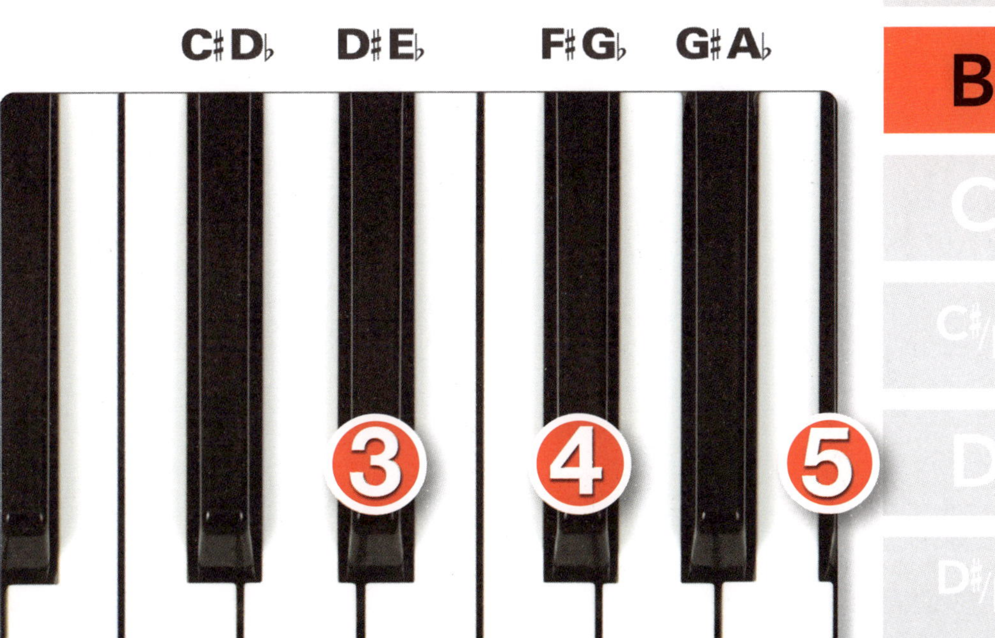

Chord Spelling

1st (B), 3rd (D♯), 5th (F♯), 7th (A♯)

Left hand suggestion: 1st (root note) and 5th

FREE ACCESS on smartphones including iPhone & Android

Using any free QR code app, scan and **HEAR** the chord

Bm7
Minor 7th

Chord Spelling

1st (B), ♭3rd (D), 5th (F#), ♭7th (A)

Left hand suggestion: 1st (root note) and 5th

FREE ACCESS on smartphones
including iPhone & Android

Using any free QR code app,
scan and **HEAR** the chord

B7
Dominant 7th

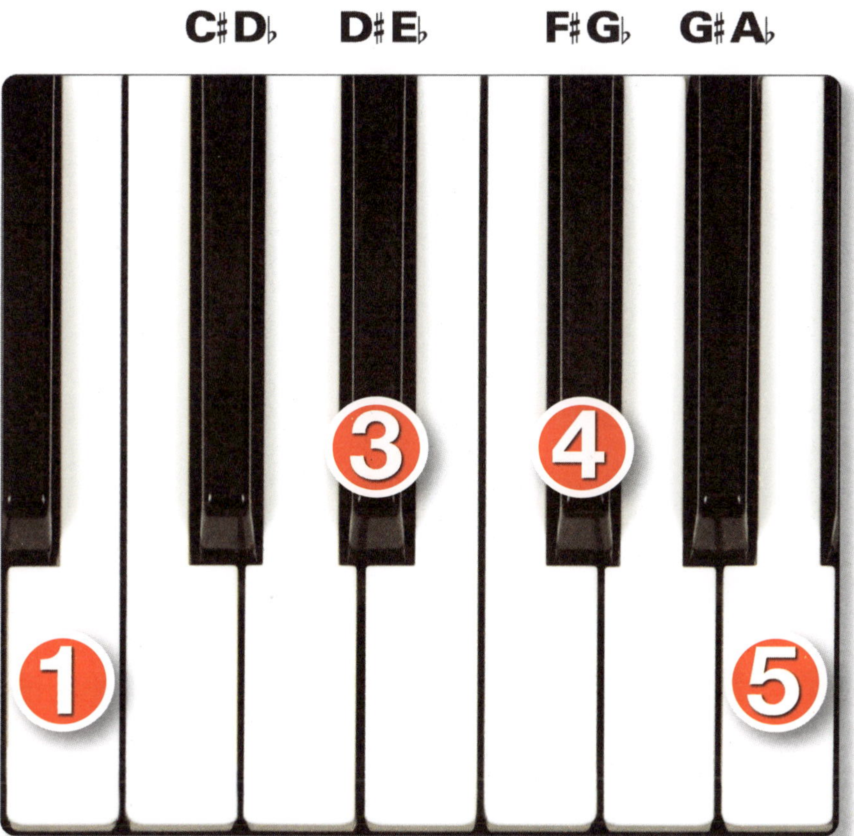

Chord Spelling

1st (B), 3rd (D♯), 5th (F♯), ♭7th (A)

Left hand suggestion: 1st (root note) and 5th

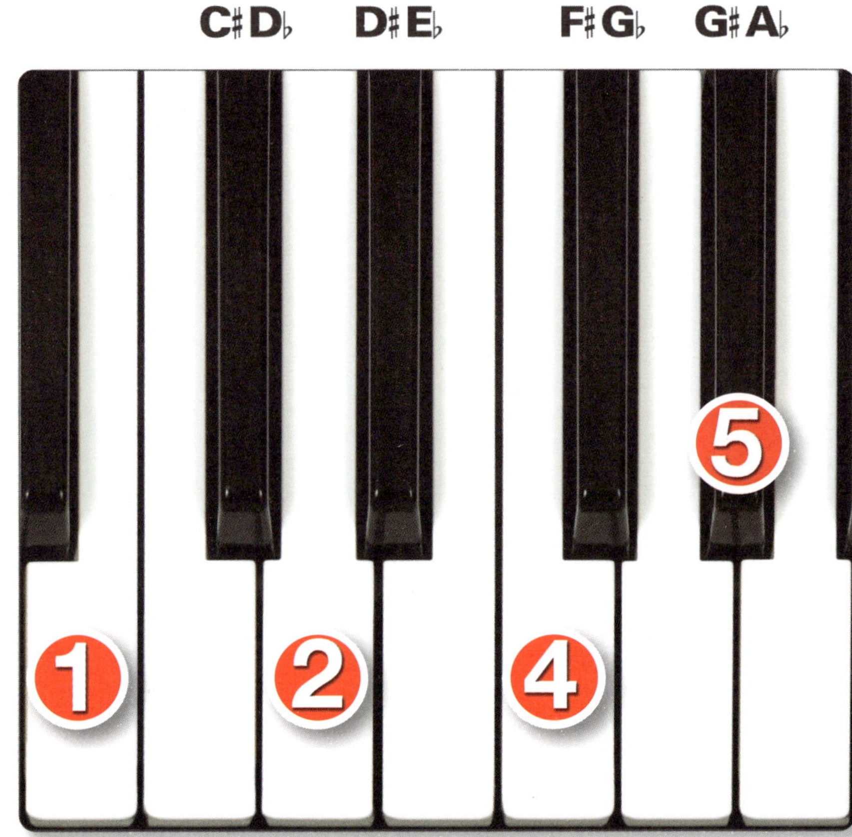

B°7
Diminished 7th

Chord Spelling

1st (B), ♭3rd (D), ♭5th (F), ♭♭7th (A♭)

Left hand suggestion: 1st (root note) and 5th

FREE ACCESS on smartphones including iPhone & Android

Using any free QR code app, scan and **HEAR** the chord

Bmaj9
Major 9th

Chord Spelling

1st (B), 3rd (D#), 5th (F#), 7th (A#), 9th (C#)

Left hand suggestion: 1st (root note) and 5th

FREE ACCESS on smartphones including iPhone & Android

Using any free QR code app, scan and **HEAR** the chord

C
Major

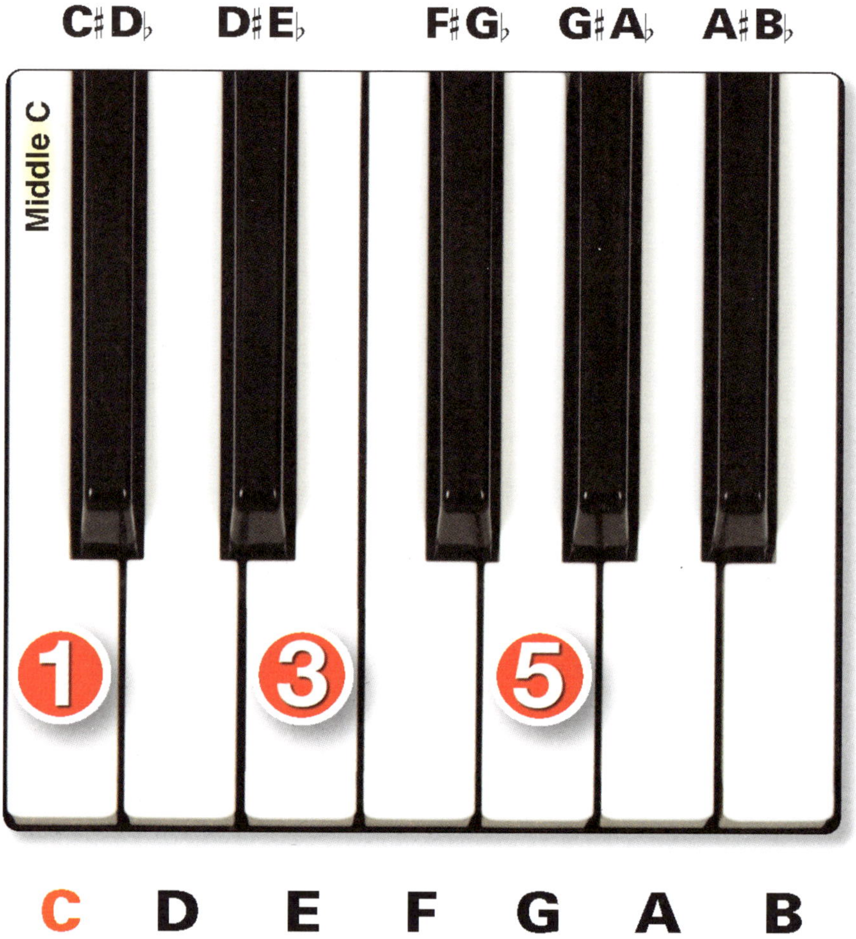

Chord Spelling

1st (C), 3rd (E), 5th (G)

Left hand suggestion: 1st (root note) and 5th

FREE ACCESS on smartphones including iPhone & Android

Using any free QR code app, scan and **HEAR** the chord

Chord Spelling

1st (C), ♭3rd (E♭), 5th (G)

Left hand suggestion: 1st (root note) and 5th

FREE ACCESS on smartphones including iPhone & Android

Using any free QR code app, scan and **HEAR** the chord

C+
Augmented Triad

Chord Spelling
1st (C), 3rd (E), ♯5th (G♯)

Left hand suggestion: 1st (root note) and 5th

FREE ACCESS on smartphones including iPhone & Android

Using any free QR code app, scan and **HEAR** the chord

C°
Diminished Triad

Chord Spelling

1st (C), ♭3rd (E♭), ♭5th (G♭)

Left hand suggestion: 1st (root note) and 5th

FREE ACCESS on smartphones including iPhone & Android

Using any free QR code app, scan and **HEAR** the chord

Csus2
Suspended 2nd

Chord Spelling

1st (C), 2nd (D), 5th (G)

Left hand suggestion: 1st (root note) and 5th

FREE ACCESS on smartphones
including iPhone & Android

Using any free QR code app,
scan and **HEAR** the chord

Csus4
Suspended 4th

Chord Spelling

1st (C), 4th (F), 5th (G)

Left hand suggestion: 1st (root note) and 5th

FREE ACCESS on smartphones including iPhone & Android

Using any free QR code app, scan and **HEAR** the chord

C5
5th (Power Chord)

Chord Spelling

1st (C), 5th (G)

Left hand suggestion: 1st (root note) and 5th

FREE ACCESS on smartphones
including iPhone & Android

Using any free QR code app,
scan and **HEAR** the chord

C6
Major 6th

Chord Spelling

1st (C), 3rd (E), 5th (G), 6th (A)

Left hand suggestion: 1st (root note) and 5th

FREE ACCESS on smartphones including iPhone & Android

Using any free QR code app, scan and **HEAR** the chord

Cm6
Minor 6th

Chord Spelling

1st (C), ♭3rd (E♭), 5th (G), 6th (A)

Left hand suggestion: 1st (root note) and 5th

FREE ACCESS on smartphones including iPhone & Android

Using any free QR code app, scan and **HEAR** the chord

Cmaj7
Major 7th

Chord Spelling

1st (C), 3rd (E), 5th (G), 7th (B)

Left hand suggestion: 1st (root note) and 5th

FREE ACCESS on smartphones including iPhone & Android

Using any free QR code app, scan and **HEAR** the chord

Cm7
Minor 7th

Chord Spelling

1st (C), ♭3rd (E♭), 5th (G), ♭7th (B♭)

Left hand suggestion: 1st (root note) and 5th

FREE ACCESS on smartphones
including iPhone & Android

Using any free QR code app,
scan and **HEAR** the chord

C7
Dominant 7th

Chord Spelling

1st (C), 3rd (E), 5th (G), ♭7th (B♭)

Left hand suggestion: 1st (root note) and 5th

FREE ACCESS on smartphones including iPhone & Android

Using any free QR code app, scan and **HEAR** the chord

C°7
Diminished 7th

Chord Spelling

1st (C), ♭3rd (E♭), ♭5th (G♭), ♭♭7th (B♭♭)

Left hand suggestion: 1st (root note) and 5th

FREE ACCESS on smartphones including iPhone & Android

Using any free QR code app, scan and **HEAR** the chord

62

Cmaj9
Major 9th

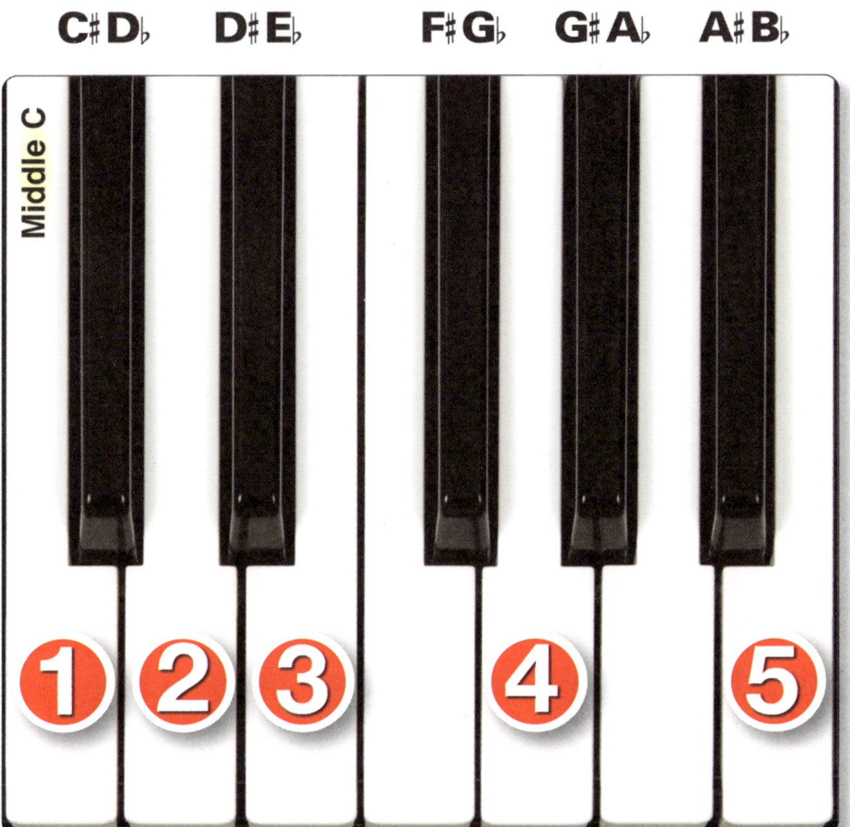

Chord Spelling

1st (C), 3rd (E), 5th (G), 7th (B), 9th (D)

Left hand suggestion: 1st (root note) and 5th

FREE ACCESS on smartphones including iPhone & Android

Using any free QR code app, scan and **HEAR** the chord

C♯/D♭
Major

Chord Spelling

1st (C♯), 3rd (E♯), 5th (G♯)

Left hand suggestion: 1st (root note) and 5th

FREE ACCESS on smartphones including iPhone & Android

Using any free QR code app, scan and **HEAR** the chord

C#/D♭m
Minor

C#D♭   **D#E♭**   **F#G♭**   **G#A♭**   **A#B♭**

Middle C

1 **2** **4**

C D E F G A B

Chord Spelling

1st (C#), ♭3rd (E), 5th (G#)

Left hand suggestion: 1st (root note) and 5th

A
A#/B♭
B
C
C#/D♭
D
D#/E♭
E
F
F#/G♭
G
G#/A♭

FREE ACCESS on smartphones
including iPhone & Android

Using any free QR code app,
scan and **HEAR** the chord

C♯/D♭+
Augmented Triad

Chord Spelling

1st (C♯), 3rd (E♯), ♯5th (Gx)

Left hand suggestion: 1st (root note) and 5th

FREE ACCESS on smartphones including iPhone & Android

Using any free QR code app, scan and **HEAR** the chord

C♯/D♭°
Diminished Triad

Chord Spelling
1st (C♯), ♭3rd (E), ♭5th (G)

Left hand suggestion: 1st (root note) and 5th

FREE ACCESS on smartphones including iPhone & Android

Using any free QR code app, scan and **HEAR** the chord

C♯/D♭sus2
Suspended 2nd

Chord Spelling

1st (C♯), 2nd (D♯), 5th (G♯)

Left hand suggestion: 1st (root note) and 5th

FREE ACCESS on smartphones including iPhone & Android

Using any free QR code app, scan and **HEAR** the chord

C#/D♭sus4
Suspended 4th

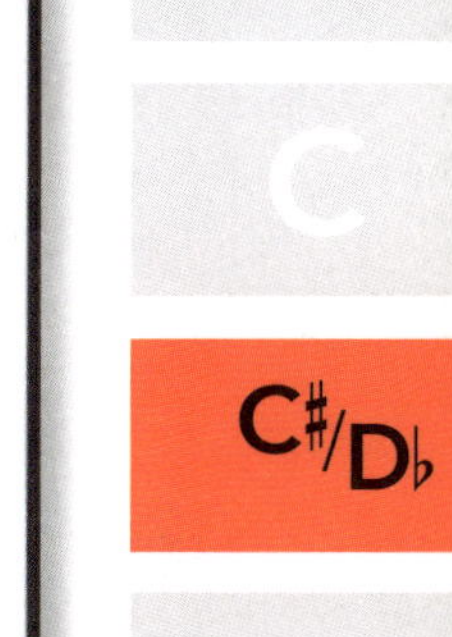

Chord Spelling

1st (C#), 4th (F#), 5th (G#)

Left hand suggestion: 1st (root note) and 5th

FREE ACCESS on smartphones including iPhone & Android

Using any free QR code app, scan and **HEAR** the chord

C#/D♭5
5th (Power Chord)

Chord Spelling

1st (C#), 5th (G#)

Left hand suggestion: 1st (root note) and 5th

FREE ACCESS on smartphones including iPhone & Android

Using any free QR code app, scan and **HEAR** the chord

Chord Spelling

1st (C#), 3rd (E#), 5th (G#), 6th (A#)

Left hand suggestion: 1st (root note) and 5th

FREE ACCESS on smartphones including iPhone & Android

Using any free QR code app, scan and **HEAR** the chord

C#/D♭m6
Minor 6th

Chord Spelling

1st (C#), ♭3rd (E), 5th (G#), 6th (A#)

Left hand suggestion: 1st (root note) and 5th

FREE ACCESS on smartphones including iPhone & Android

Using any free QR code app, scan and **HEAR** the chord

C♯/D♭maj7
Major 7th

Chord Spelling

1st (C♯), 3rd (E♯), 5th (G♯), 7th (B♯)

Left hand suggestion: 1st (root note) and 5th

FREE ACCESS on smartphones including iPhone & Android

Using any free QR code app, scan and **HEAR** the chord

C♯/D♭m7
Minor 7th

Chord Spelling

1st (C♯), ♭3rd (E), 5th (G♯), ♭7th (B)

Left hand suggestion: 1st (root note) and 5th

FREE ACCESS on smartphones including iPhone & Android

Using any free QR code app, scan and **HEAR** the chord

C♯/D♭7
Dominant 7th

Chord Spelling

1st (C♯), 3rd (E♯), 5th (G♯), ♭7th (B)

Left hand suggestion: 1st (root note) and 5th

FREE ACCESS on smartphones including iPhone & Android

Using any free QR code app, scan and **HEAR** the chord

C♯/D♭°7
Diminished 7th

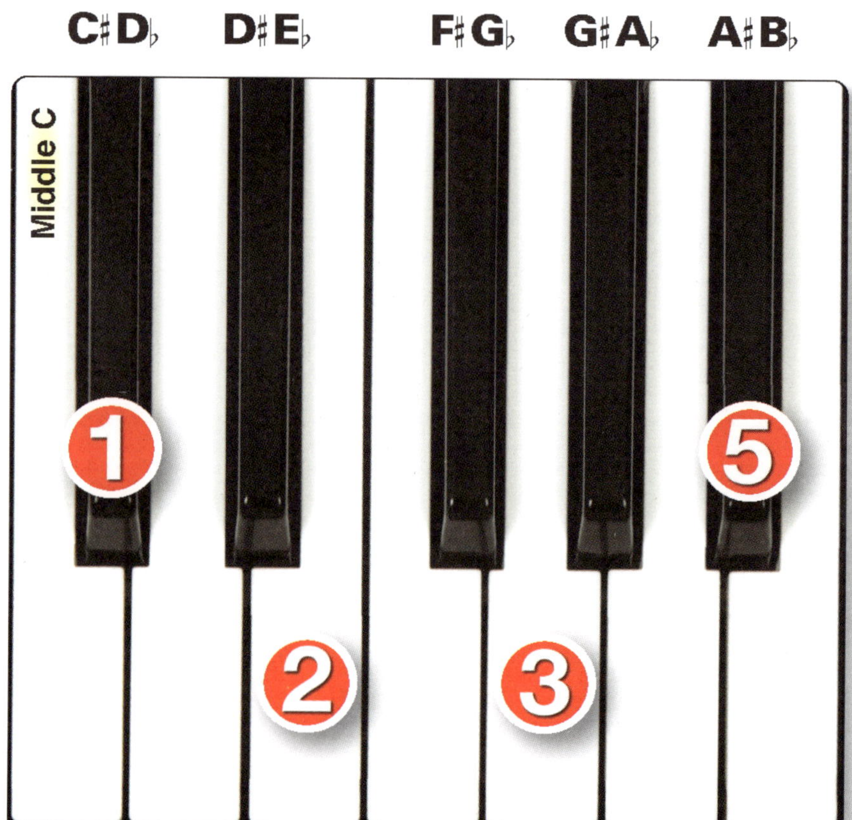

Chord Spelling

1st (C♯), ♭3rd (E), ♭5th (G), ♭♭7th (B♭)

Left hand suggestion: 1st (root note) and 5th

FREE ACCESS on smartphones including iPhone & Android

Using any free QR code app, scan and **HEAR** the chord

C♯/D♭maj9
Major 9th

Chord Spelling

1st (C♯), 3rd (E♯), 5th (G♯), 7th (B♯), 9th (D♯)

Left hand suggestion: 1st (root note) and 5th

FREE ACCESS on smartphones
including iPhone & Android

Using any free QR code app,
scan and **HEAR** the chord

D
Major

Chord Spelling

1st (D), 3rd (F♯), 5th (A)

Left hand suggestion: 1st (root note) and 5th

FREE ACCESS on smartphones including iPhone & Android

Using any free QR code app, scan and **HEAR** the chord

Dm
Minor

Chord Spelling

1st (D), ♭3rd (F), 5th (A)

Left hand suggestion: 1st (root note) and 5th

FREE ACCESS on smartphones
including iPhone & Android

Using any free QR code app,
scan and **HEAR** the chord

D+
Augmented Triad

Chord Spelling

1st (D), 3rd (F♯), ♯5th (A♯)

Left hand suggestion: 1st (root note) and 5th

FREE ACCESS on smartphones including iPhone & Android

Using any free QR code app, scan and **HEAR** the chord

D°
Diminished Triad

Chord Spelling

1st (D), ♭3rd (F), ♭5th (A♭)

Left hand suggestion: 1st (root note) and 5th

FREE ACCESS on smartphones including iPhone & Android

Using any free QR code app, scan and **HEAR** the chord

Dsus2
Suspended 2nd

Chord Spelling

1st (D), 2nd (E), 5th (A)

Left hand suggestion: 1st (root note) and 5th

FREE ACCESS on smartphones including iPhone & Android

Using any free QR code app, scan and **HEAR** the chord

Dsus4
Suspended 4th

Chord Spelling

1st (D), 4th (G), 5th (A)

Left hand suggestion: 1st (root note) and 5th

FREE ACCESS on smartphones including iPhone & Android

Using any free QR code app, scan and **HEAR** the chord

D5
5th (Power Chord)

Chord Spelling
1st (D), 5th (A)

Left hand suggestion: 1st (root note) and 5th

D6
Major 6th

Chord Spelling

1st (D), 3rd (F♯), 5th (A), 6th (B)

Left hand suggestion: 1st (root note) and 5th

FREE ACCESS on smartphones
including iPhone & Android

Using any free QR code app,
scan and **HEAR** the chord

Dm6
Minor 6th

Chord Spelling

1st (D), ♭3rd (F), 5th (A), 6th (B)

Left hand suggestion: 1st (root note) and 5th

FREE ACCESS on smartphones including iPhone & Android

Using any free QR code app, scan and **HEAR** the chord

86

Dmaj7
Major 7th

Chord Spelling

1st (D), 3rd (F♯), 5th (A), 7th (C♯)

Left hand suggestion: 1st (root note) and 5th

FREE ACCESS on smartphones including iPhone & Android

Using any free QR code app, scan and **HEAR** the chord

Dm7
Minor 7th

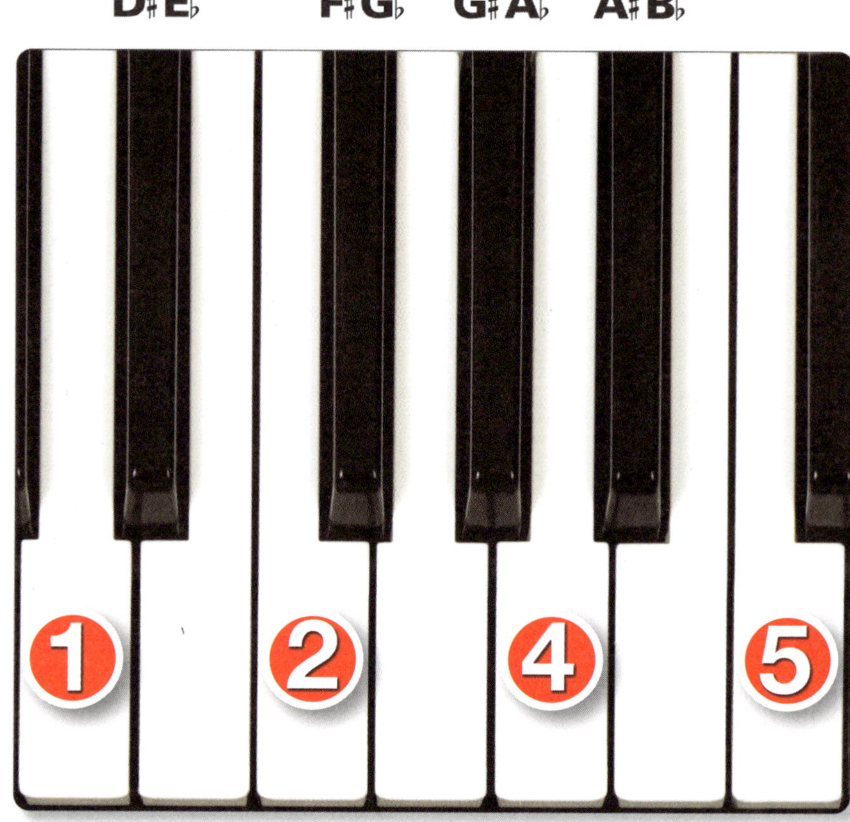

Chord Spelling

1st (D), ♭3rd (F), 5th (A), ♭7th (C)

Left hand suggestion: 1st (root note) and 5th

FREE ACCESS on smartphones
including iPhone & Android

Using any free QR code app,
scan and **HEAR** the chord

D7
Dominant 7th

Chord Spelling

1st (D), 3rd (F#), 5th (A), ♭7th (C)

Left hand suggestion: 1st (root note) and 5th

FREE ACCESS on smartphones
including iPhone & Android

Using any free QR code app,
scan and **HEAR** the chord

D°7
Diminished 7th

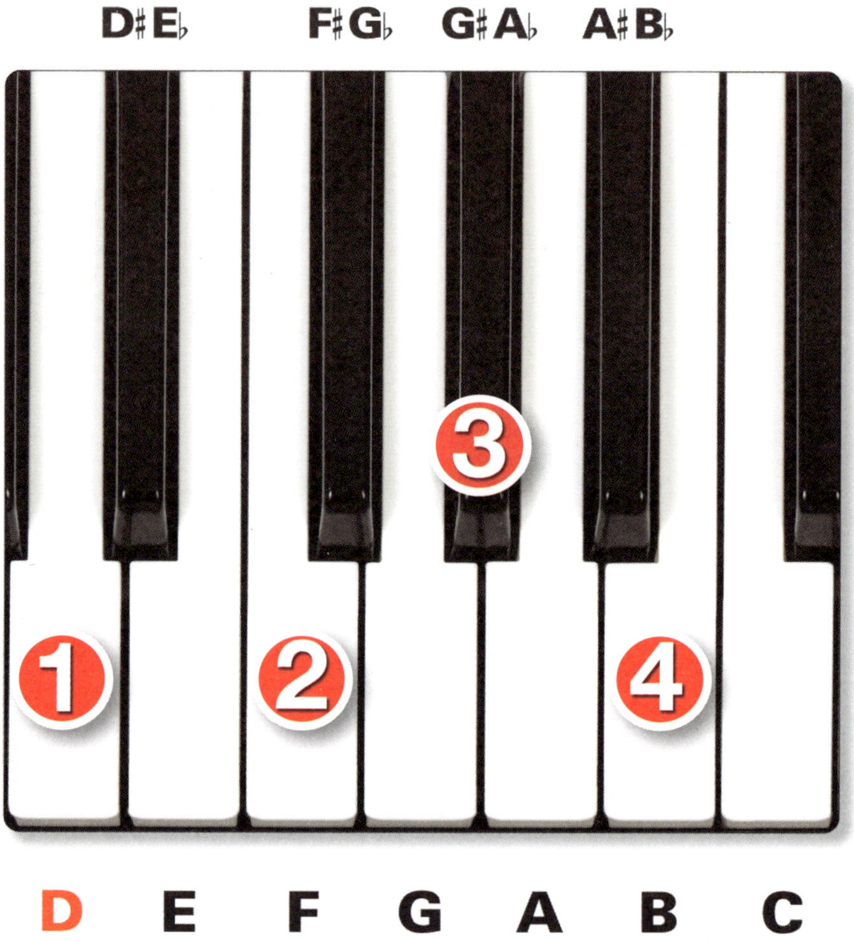

Chord Spelling

1st (D), ♭3rd (F), ♭5th (A♭), ♭♭7th (B)

Left hand suggestion: 1st (root note) and 5th

FREE ACCESS on smartphones
including iPhone & Android

Using any free QR code app,
scan and **HEAR** the chord

Dmaj9
Major 9th

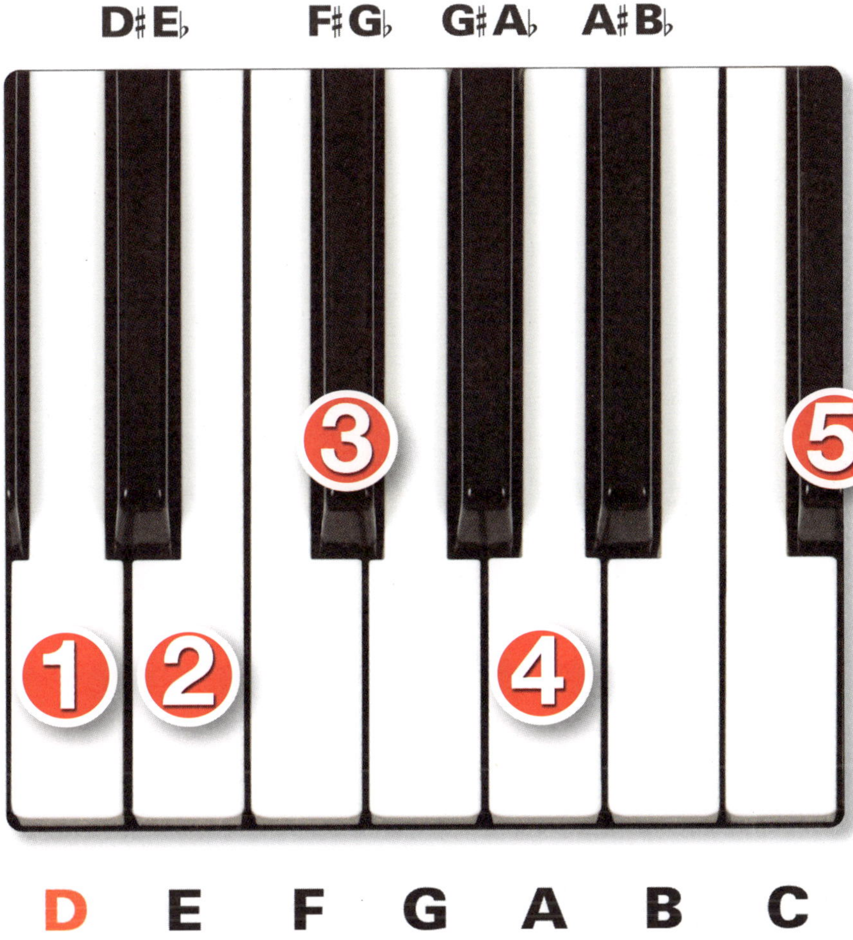

Chord Spelling

1st (D), 3rd (F#), 5th (A), 7th (C#), 9th (E)

Left hand suggestion: 1st (root note) and 5th

FREE ACCESS on smartphones
including iPhone & Android

Using any free QR code app,
scan and **HEAR** the chord

D♯/E♭
Major

Chord Spelling

1st (E♭), 3rd (G), 5th (B♭)

Left hand suggestion: 1st (root note) and 5th

FREE ACCESS on smartphones including iPhone & Android

Using any free QR code app, scan and **HEAR** the chord

D♯/E♭m
Minor

Chord Spelling

1st (E♭), ♭3rd (G♭), 5th (B♭)

Left hand suggestion: 1st (root note) and 5th

FREE ACCESS on smartphones
including iPhone & Android

Using any free QR code app,
scan and **HEAR** the chord

D♯/E♭+

Augmented Triad

Chord Spelling

1st (E♭), 3rd (G), ♯5th (B)

Left hand suggestion: 1st (root note) and 5th

FREE ACCESS on smartphones including iPhone & Android

Using any free QR code app, scan and **HEAR** the chord

D♯/E♭°
Diminished Triad

Chord Spelling

1st (E♭), ♭3rd (G♭), ♭5th (B♭♭)

Left hand suggestion: 1st (root note) and 5th

FREE ACCESS on smartphones including iPhone & Android

Using any free QR code app, scan and **HEAR** the chord

D♯/E♭sus2
Suspended 2nd

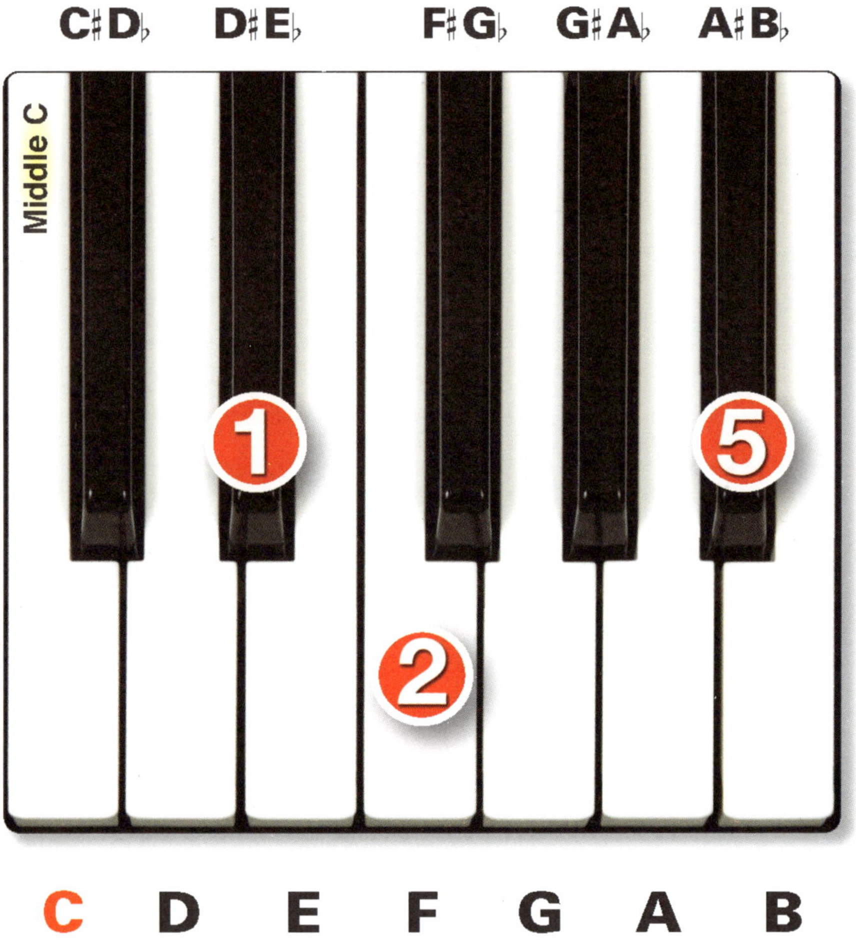

Chord Spelling

1st (E♭), 2nd (F), 5th (B♭)

Left hand suggestion: 1st (root note) and 5th

FREE ACCESS on smartphones
including iPhone & Android

Using any free QR code app,
scan and **HEAR** the chord

D♯/E♭sus4
Suspended 4th

Chord Spelling
1st (E♭), 4th (A♭), 5th (B♭)

Left hand suggestion: 1st (root note) and 5th

FREE ACCESS on smartphones including iPhone & Android

Using any free QR code app, scan and **HEAR** the chord

D♯/E♭5
5th (Power Chord)

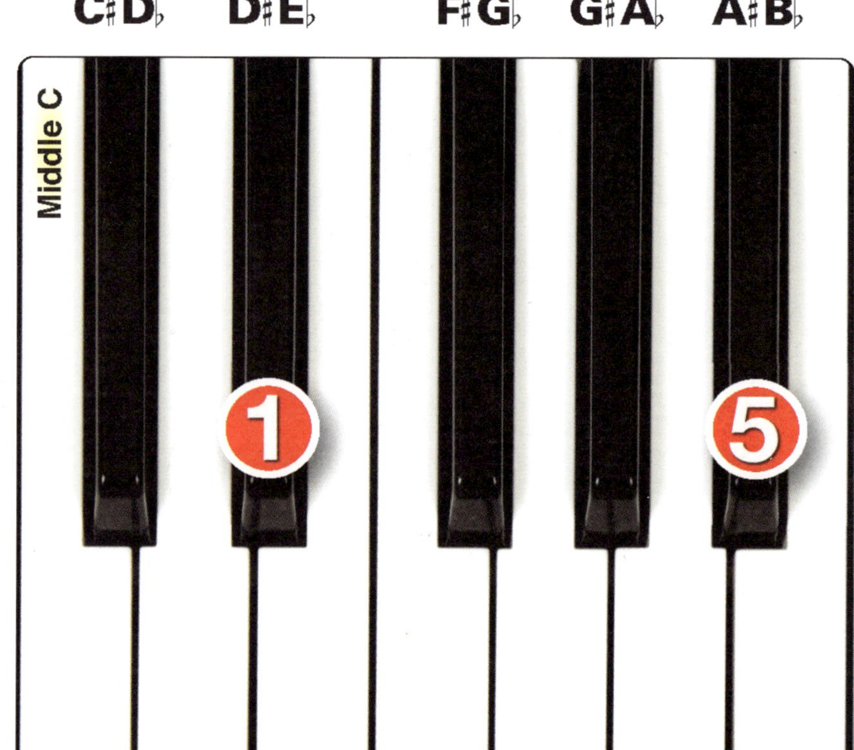

Chord Spelling

1st (E♭), 5th (B♭)

Left hand suggestion: 1st (root note) and 5th

FREE ACCESS on smartphones
including iPhone & Android

Using any free QR code app,
scan and **HEAR** the chord

D♯/E♭6
Major 6th

Chord Spelling

1st (E♭), 3rd (G), 5th (B♭), 6th (C)

Left hand suggestion: 1st (root note) and 5th

FREE ACCESS on smartphones including iPhone & Android

Using any free QR code app, scan and **HEAR** the chord

D#/E♭m6
Minor 6th

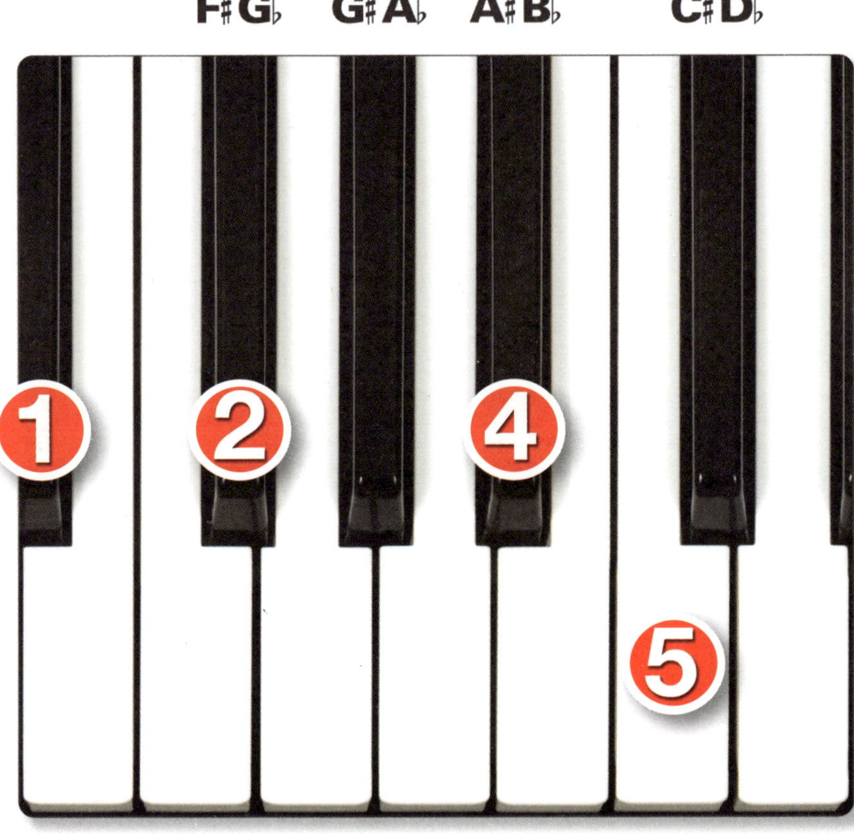

Chord Spelling

1st (E♭), ♭3rd (G♭), 5th (B♭), 6th (C)

Left hand suggestion: 1st (root note) and 5th

FREE ACCESS on smartphones including iPhone & Android

Using any free QR code app, scan and **HEAR** the chord

D♯/E♭maj7
Major 7th

Chord Spelling

1st (E♭), 3rd (G), 5th (B♭), 7th (D)

Left hand suggestion: 1st (root note) and 5th

FREE ACCESS on smartphones including iPhone & Android

Using any free QR code app, scan and **HEAR** the chord

D♯/E♭m7
Minor 7th

Chord Spelling

1st (E♭), ♭3rd (G♭), 5th (B♭), ♭7th (D♭)

Left hand suggestion: 1st (root note) and 5th

FREE ACCESS on smartphones
including iPhone & Android

Using any free QR code app,
scan and **HEAR** the chord

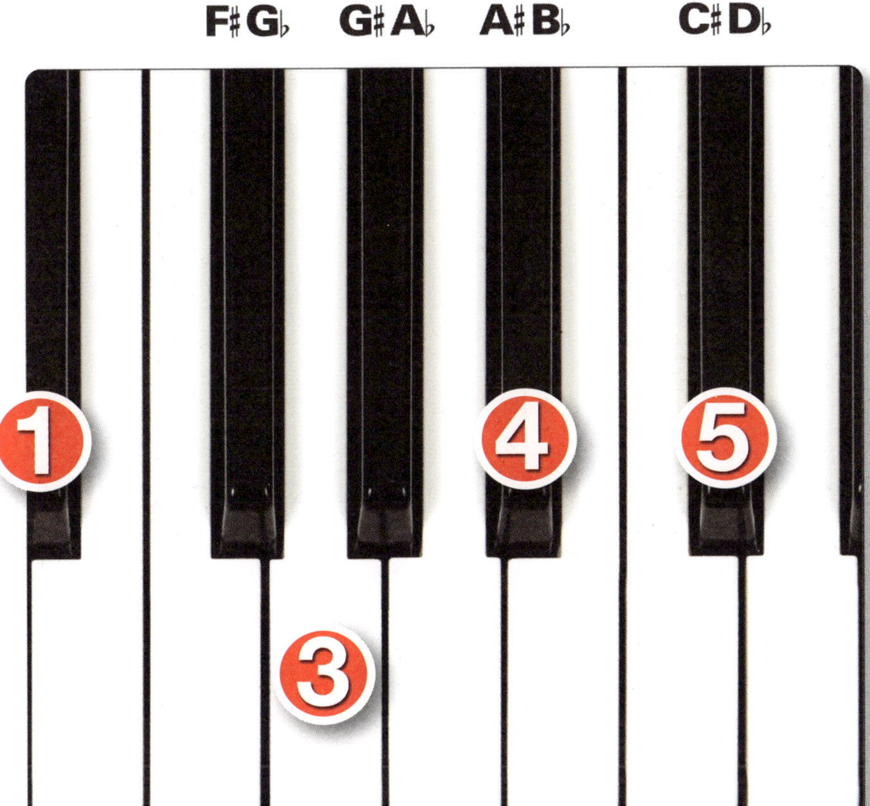

D#/Eb7
Dominant 7th

Chord Spelling

1st (Eb), 3rd (G), 5th (Bb), b7th (Db)

Left hand suggestion: 1st (root note) and 5th

FREE ACCESS on smartphones including iPhone & Android

Using any free QR code app, scan and **HEAR** the chord

D♯/E♭°7
Diminished 7th

Chord Spelling

1st (E♭), ♭3rd (G♭), ♭5th (B♭♭), ♭♭7th (D♭♭)

Left hand suggestion: 1st (root note) and 5th

FREE ACCESS on smartphones including iPhone & Android

Using any free QR code app, scan and **HEAR** the chord

D♯/E♭maj9
Major 9th

Chord Spelling

1st (E♭), 3rd (G), 5th (B♭), 7th (D), 9th (F)

Left hand suggestion: 1st (root note) and 5th

FREE ACCESS on smartphones including iPhone & Android

Using any free QR code app, scan and **HEAR** the chord

E
Major

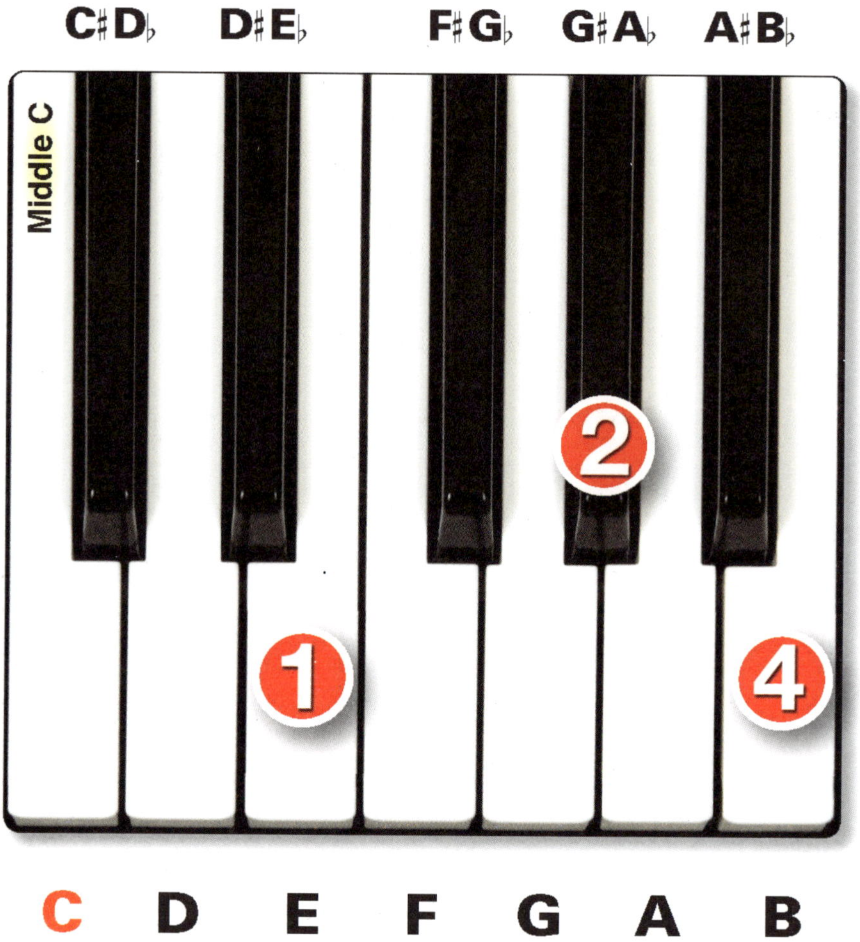

Chord Spelling

1st (E), 3rd (G♯), 5th (B)

Left hand suggestion: 1st (root note) and 5th

FREE ACCESS on smartphones including iPhone & Android

Using any free QR code app, scan and **HEAR** the chord

Em
Minor

Chord Spelling

1st (E), ♭3rd (G), 5th (B)

Left hand suggestion: 1st (root note) and 5th

FREE ACCESS on smartphones including iPhone & Android

Using any free QR code app, scan and **HEAR** the chord

E+
Augmented Triad

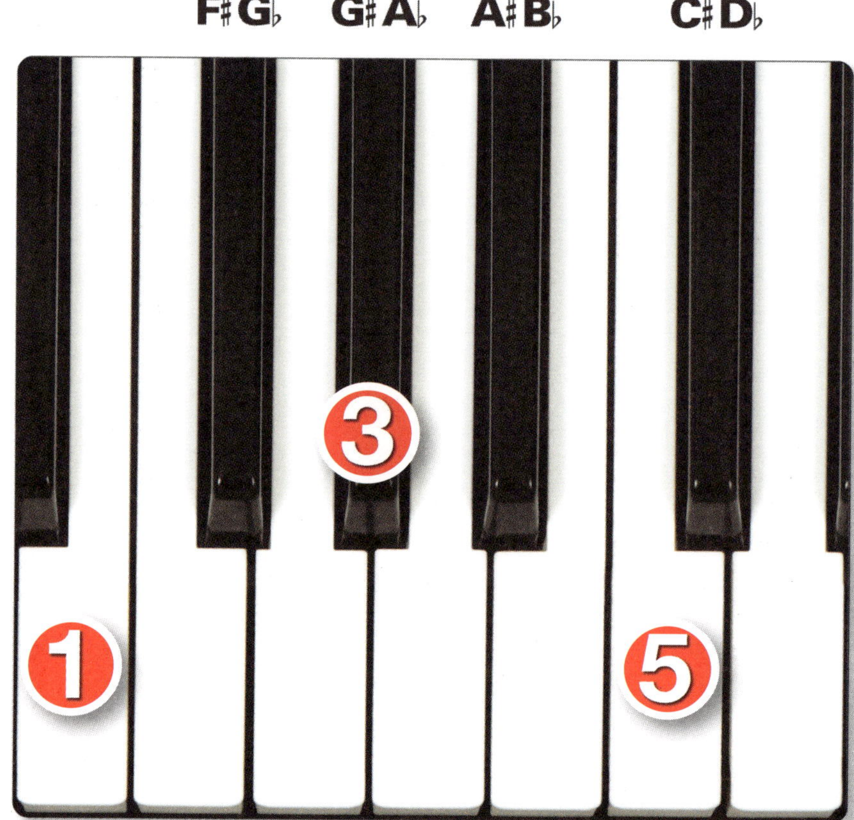

Chord Spelling

1st (E), 3rd (G#), #5th (B#)

Left hand suggestion: 1st (root note) and 5th

E°
Diminished Triad

Chord Spelling
1st (E), ♭3rd (G), ♭5th (B♭)

Left hand suggestion: 1st (root note) and 5th

FREE ACCESS on smartphones
including iPhone & Android

Using any free QR code app,
scan and **HEAR** the chord

Esus2
Suspended 2nd

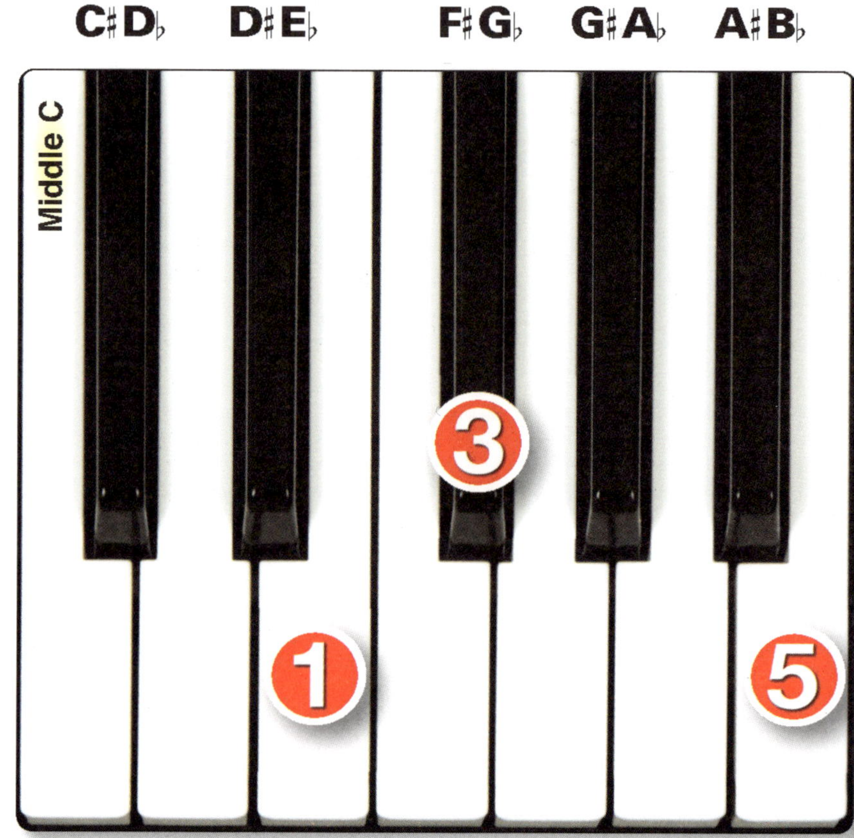

Chord Spelling

1st (E), 2nd (F♯), 5th (B)

Left hand suggestion: 1st (root note) and 5th

Esus4
Suspended 4th

Chord Spelling

1st (E), 4th (A), 5th (B)

Left hand suggestion: 1st (root note) and 5th

FREE ACCESS on smartphones including iPhone & Android

Using any free QR code app, scan and **HEAR** the chord

E5
5th (Power Chord)

Chord Spelling

1st (E), 5th (B)

Left hand suggestion: 1st (root note) and 5th

FREE ACCESS on smartphones
including iPhone & Android

Using any free QR code app,
scan and **HEAR** the chord

E6
Major 6th

Chord Spelling

1st (E), 3rd (G#), 5th (B), 6th (C#)

Left hand suggestion: 1st (root note) and 5th

FREE ACCESS on smartphones
including iPhone & Android

Using any free QR code app,
scan and **HEAR** the chord

Em6
Minor 6th

Chord Spelling

1st (E), ♭3rd (G), 5th (B), 6th (C♯)

Left hand suggestion: 1st (root note) and 5th

FREE ACCESS on smartphones including iPhone & Android

Using any free QR code app, scan and **HEAR** the chord

Emaj7
Major 7th

Chord Spelling

1st (E), 3rd (G#), 5th (B), 7th (D#)

Left hand suggestion: 1st (root note) and 5th

FREE ACCESS on smartphones including iPhone & Android

Using any free QR code app, scan and **HEAR** the chord

Em7
Minor 7th

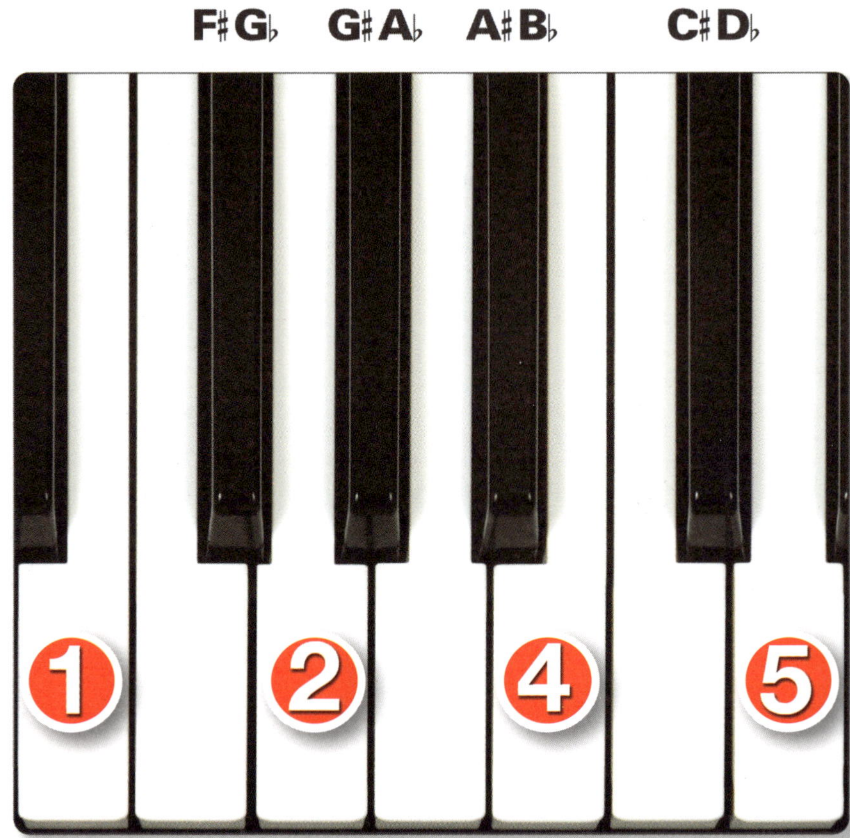

Chord Spelling

1st (E), ♭3rd (G), 5th (B), ♭7th (D)

Left hand suggestion: 1st (root note) and 5th

FREE ACCESS on smartphones including iPhone & Android

Using any free QR code app, scan and **HEAR** the chord

E7
Dominant 7th

Chord Spelling

1st (E), 3rd (G#), 5th (B), ♭7th (D)

Left hand suggestion: 1st (root note) and 5th

FREE ACCESS on smartphones including iPhone & Android

Using any free QR code app, scan and **HEAR** the chord

E°7
Diminished 7th

Chord Spelling

1st (E), ♭3rd (G), ♭5th (B♭), ♭♭7th (D♭)

Left hand suggestion: 1st (root note) and 5th

FREE ACCESS on smartphones including iPhone & Android

Using any free QR code app, scan and **HEAR** the chord

Emaj9
Major 9th

Chord Spelling

1st (E), 3rd (G#), 5th (B), 7th (D#), 9th (F#)

Left hand suggestion: 1st (root note) and 5th

FREE ACCESS on smartphones including iPhone & Android

Using any free QR code app, scan and **HEAR** the chord

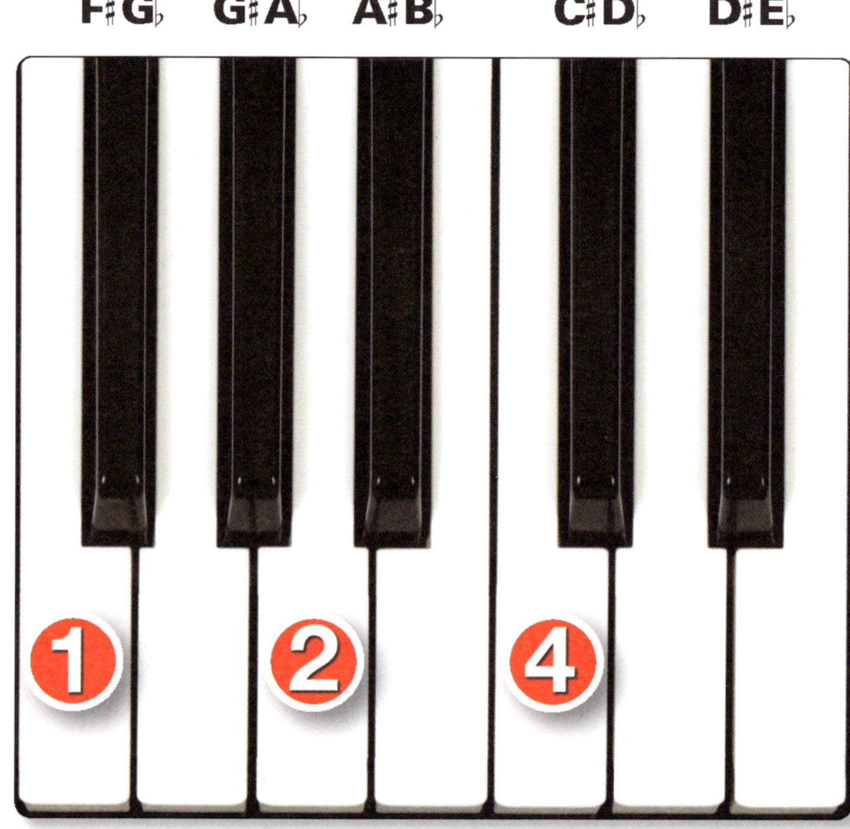

F
Major

Chord Spelling
1st (F), 3rd (A), 5th (C)

Left hand suggestion: 1st (root note) and 5th

FREE ACCESS on smartphones including iPhone & Android

Using any free QR code app, scan and **HEAR** the chord

Fm
Minor

Chord Spelling

1st (F), ♭3rd (A♭), 5th (C)

Left hand suggestion: 1st (root note) and 5th

FREE ACCESS on smartphones including iPhone & Android

Using any free QR code app, scan and **HEAR** the chord

F+
Augmented Triad

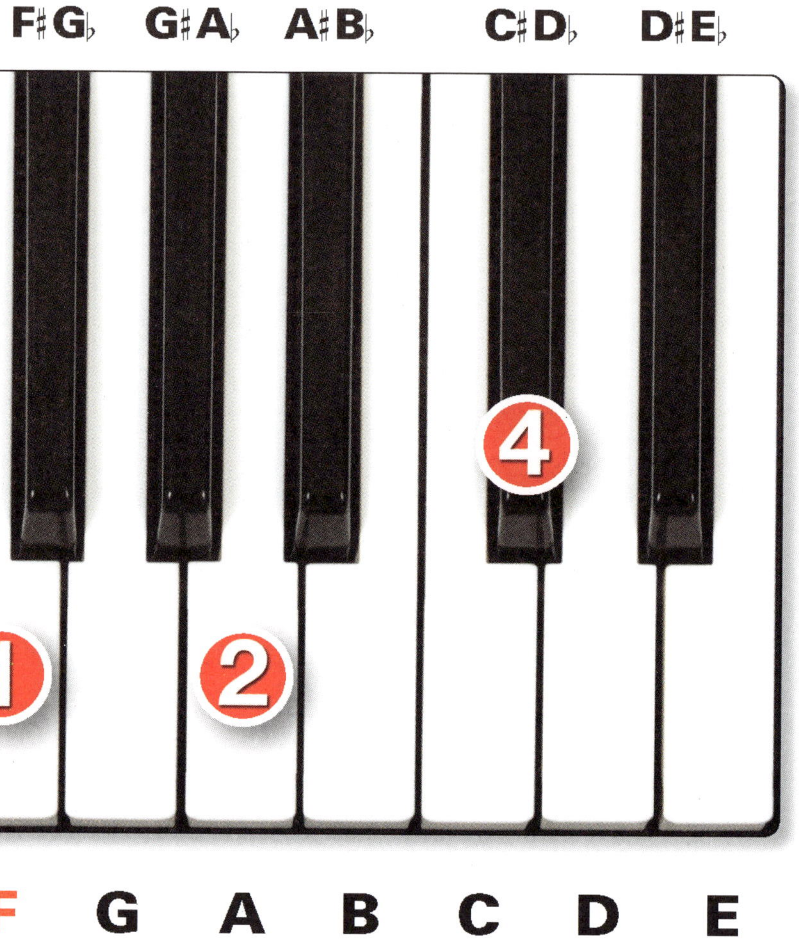

Chord Spelling
1st (F), 3rd (A), ♯5th (C♯)

Left hand suggestion: 1st (root note) and 5th

FREE ACCESS on smartphones
including iPhone & Android

Using any free QR code app,
scan and **HEAR** the chord

F°
Diminished Triad

Chord Spelling

1st (F), ♭3rd (A♭), ♭5th (C♭)

Left hand suggestion: 1st (root note) and 5th

FREE ACCESS on smartphones
including iPhone & Android

Using any free QR code app,
scan and **HEAR** the chord

Fsus2
Suspended 2nd

Chord Spelling

1st (F), 2nd (G), 5th (C)

Left hand suggestion: 1st (root note) and 5th

FREE ACCESS on smartphones including iPhone & Android

Using any free QR code app, scan and **HEAR** the chord

Fsus4
Suspended 4th

Chord Spelling

1st (F), 4th (B♭), 5th (C)

Left hand suggestion: 1st (root note) and 5th

FREE ACCESS on smartphones
including iPhone & Android

Using any free QR code app,
scan and **HEAR** the chord

F5
5th (Power Chord)

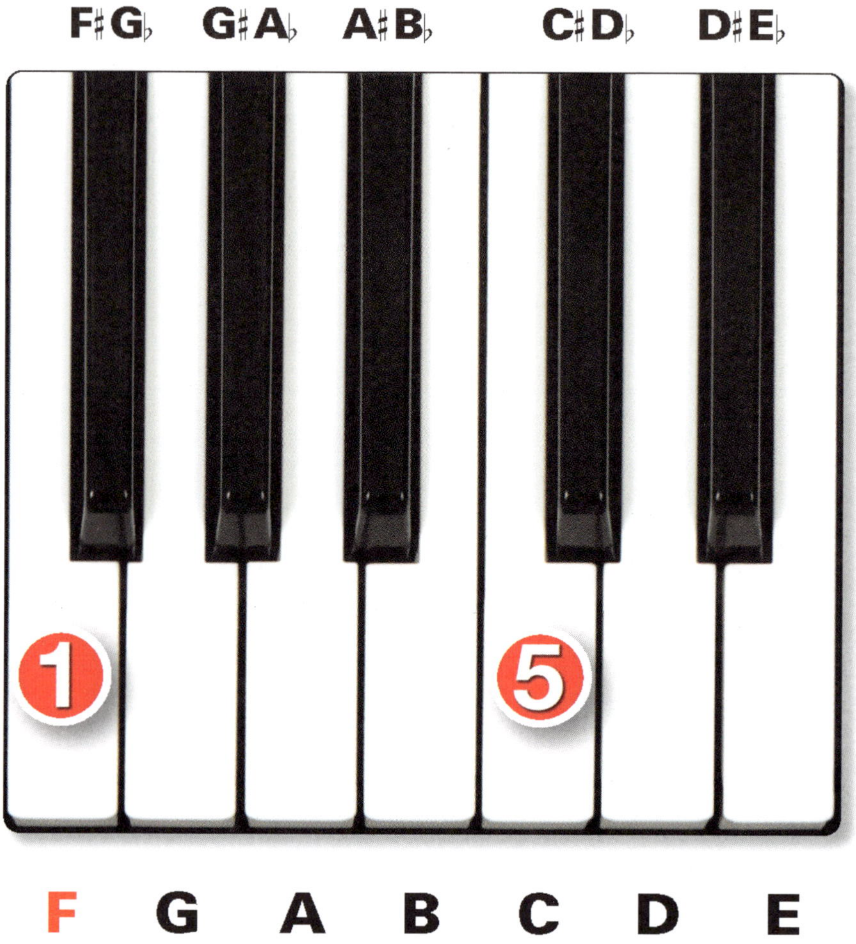

Chord Spelling

1st (F), 5th (C)

Left hand suggestion: 1st (root note) and 5th

FREE ACCESS on smartphones including iPhone & Android

Using any free QR code app, scan and **HEAR** the chord

F6
Major 6th

Chord Spelling

1st (F), 3rd (A), 5th (C), 6th (D)

Left hand suggestion: 1st (root note) and 5th

FREE ACCESS on smartphones including iPhone & Android

Using any free QR code app, scan and **HEAR** the chord

Fm6
Minor 6th

Chord Spelling

1st (F), ♭3rd (A♭), 5th (C), 6th (D)

Left hand suggestion: 1st (root note) and 5th

FREE ACCESS on smartphones including iPhone & Android

Using any free QR code app, scan and **HEAR** the chord

Fmaj7
Major 7th

Chord Spelling

1st (F), 3rd (A), 5th (C), 7th (E)

Left hand suggestion: 1st (root note) and 5th

FREE ACCESS on smartphones
including iPhone & Android

Using any free QR code app,
scan and **HEAR** the chord

Fm7

Minor 7th

F♯G♭
G♯A♭
A♯B♭
C♯D♭
D♯E♭
2
5
1
4
F
G
A
B
C
D
E

Chord Spelling

1st (F), ♭3rd (A♭), 5th (C), ♭7th (E♭)

Left hand suggestion: 1st (root note) and 5th

FREE ACCESS on smartphones including iPhone & Android

Using any free QR code app, scan and **HEAR** the chord

F7
Dominant 7th

Chord Spelling

1st (F), 3rd (A), 5th (C), ♭7th (E♭)

Left hand suggestion: 1st (root note) and 5th

FREE ACCESS on smartphones including iPhone & Android

Using any free QR code app, scan and **HEAR** the chord

F°7
Diminished 7th

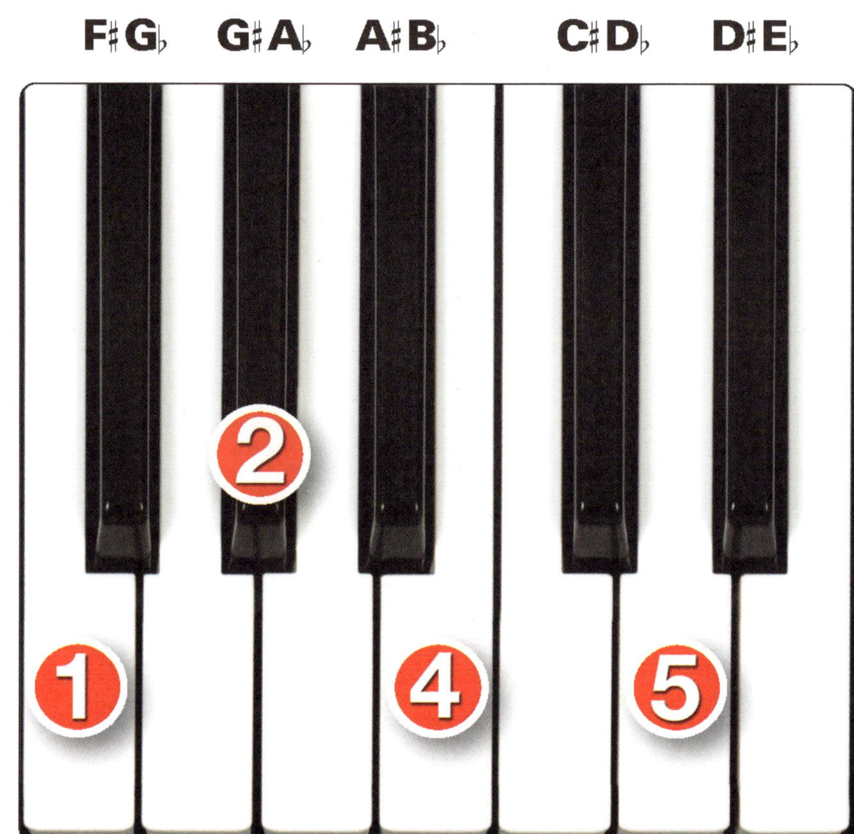

Chord Spelling

1st (F), ♭3rd (A♭), ♭5th (C♭), ♭♭7th (E♭♭)

Left hand suggestion: 1st (root note) and 5th

FREE ACCESS on smartphones including iPhone & Android

Using any free QR code app, scan and **HEAR** the chord

Fmaj9
Major 9th

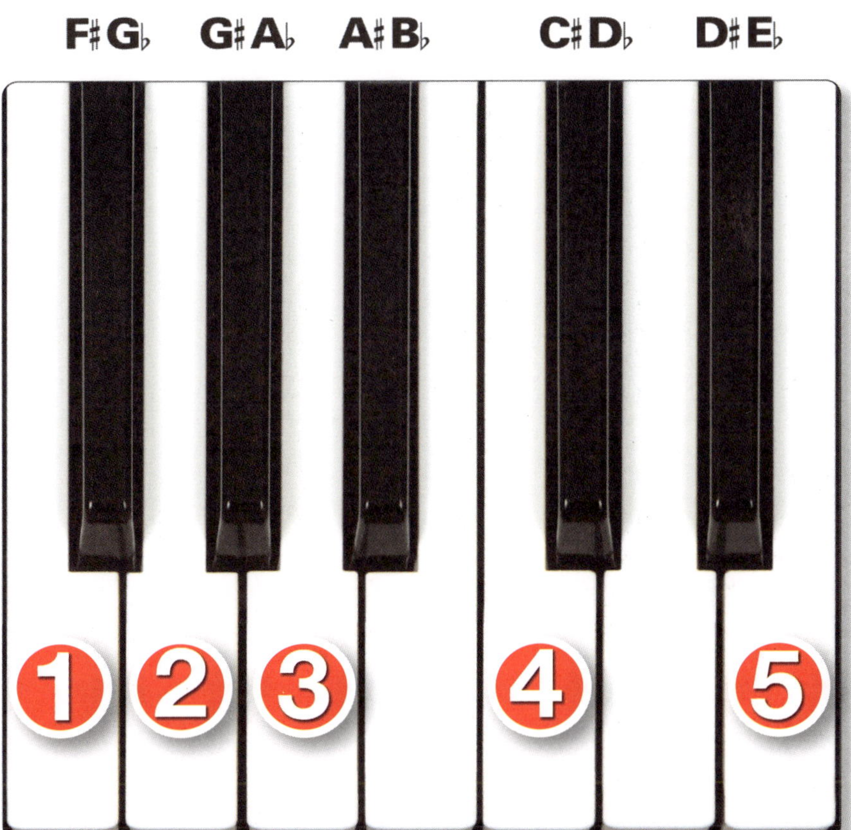

Chord Spelling

1st (F), 3rd (A), 5th (C), 7th (E), 9th (G)

Left hand suggestion: 1st (root note) and 5th

FREE ACCESS on smartphones including iPhone & Android

Using any free QR code app, scan and **HEAR** the chord

F♯/G♭ Major

Chord Spelling

1st (F♯), 3rd (A♯), 5th (C♯)

Left hand suggestion: 1st (root note) and 5th

FREE ACCESS on smartphones
including iPhone & Android

Using any free QR code app,
scan and **HEAR** the chord

Chord Spelling

1st (F♯), ♭3rd (A), 5th (C♯)

Left hand suggestion: 1st (root note) and 5th

FREE ACCESS on smartphones
including iPhone & Android

Using any free QR code app,
scan and **HEAR** the chord

F♯/G♭+
Augmented Triad

F♯G♭ G♯A♭ A♯B♭ C♯D♭ D♯E♭

F G A B C D E

F♯/G♭

Chord Spelling
1st (F♯), 3rd (A♯), ♯5th (Cx)

Left hand suggestion: 1st (root note) and 5th

FREE ACCESS on smartphones including iPhone & Android

Using any free QR code app, scan and **HEAR** the chord

F♯/G♭°
Diminished Triad

Chord Spelling

1st (F♯), ♭3rd (A), ♭5th (C)

Left hand suggestion: 1st (root note) and 5th

FREE ACCESS on smartphones including iPhone & Android

Using any free QR code app, scan and **HEAR** the chord

F♯/G♭sus2
Suspended 2nd

Chord Spelling

1st (F♯), 2nd (G♯), 5th (C♯)

Left hand suggestion: 1st (root note) and 5th

FREE ACCESS on smartphones including iPhone & Android

Using any free QR code app, scan and **HEAR** the chord

F#/G♭sus4
Suspended 4th

Chord Spelling

1st (F#), 4th (B), 5th (C#)

Left hand suggestion: 1st (root note) and 5th

FREE ACCESS on smartphones including iPhone & Android

Using any free QR code app, scan and **HEAR** the chord

F♯/G♭5
5th (Power Chord)

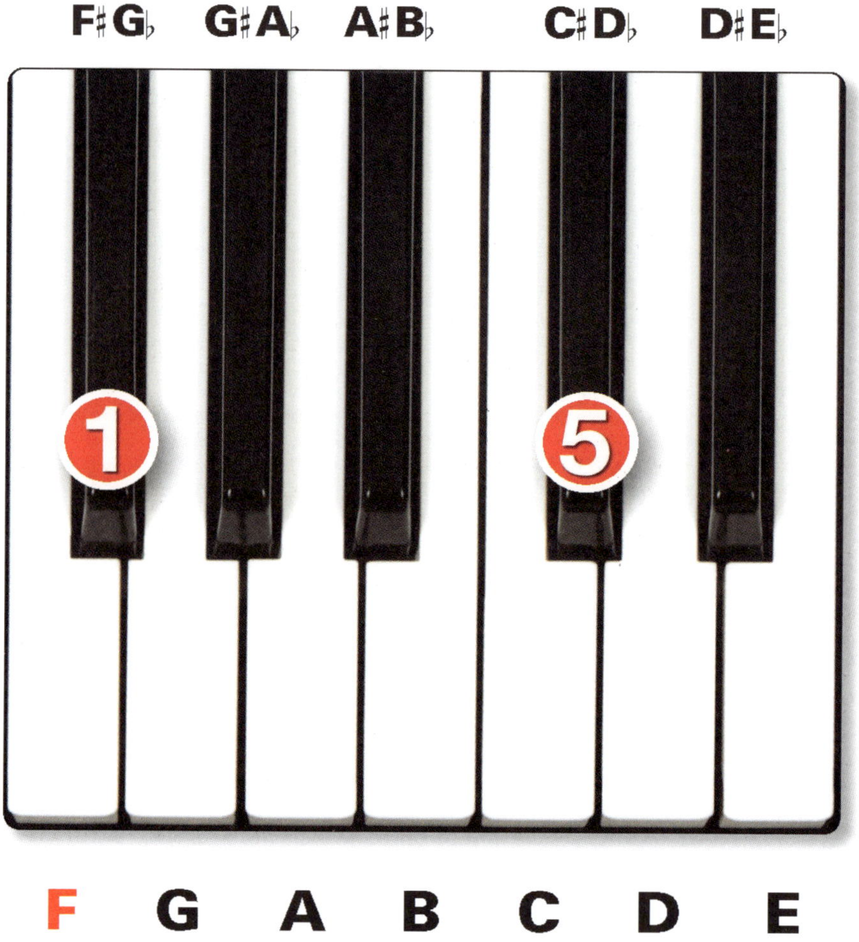

Chord Spelling

1st (F♯), 5th (C♯)

Left hand suggestion: 1st (root note) and 5th

FREE ACCESS on smartphones including iPhone & Android

Using any free QR code app, scan and **HEAR** the chord

F♯/G♭6
Major 6th

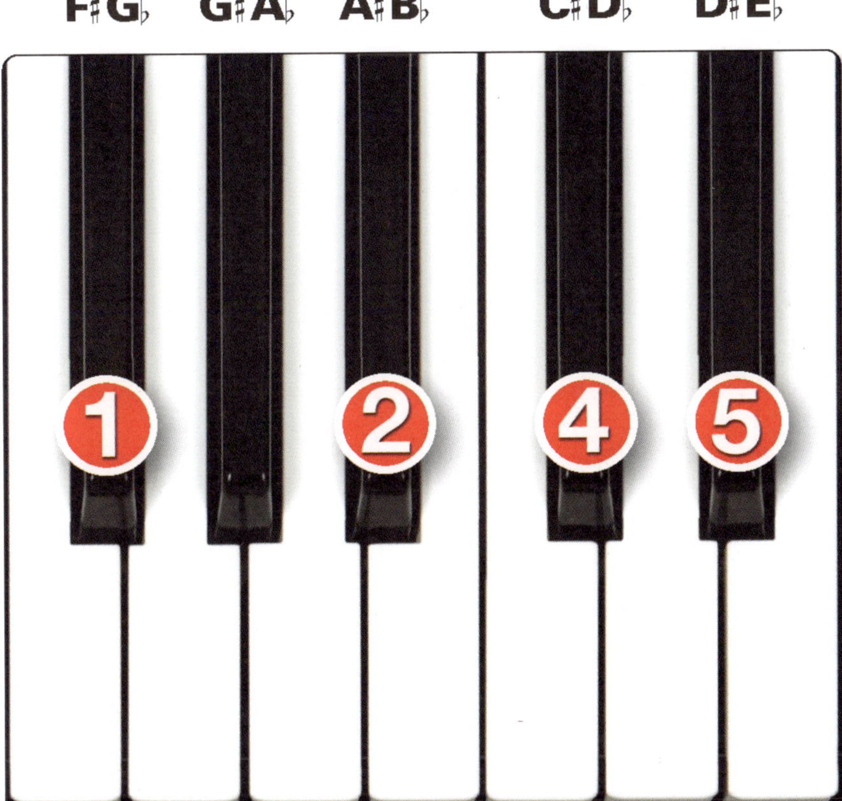

Chord Spelling

1st (F♯), 3rd (A♯), 5th (C♯), 6th (D♯)

Left hand suggestion: 1st (root note) and 5th

FREE ACCESS on smartphones including iPhone & Android

Using any free QR code app, scan and **HEAR** the chord

F♯/G♭m6
Minor 6th

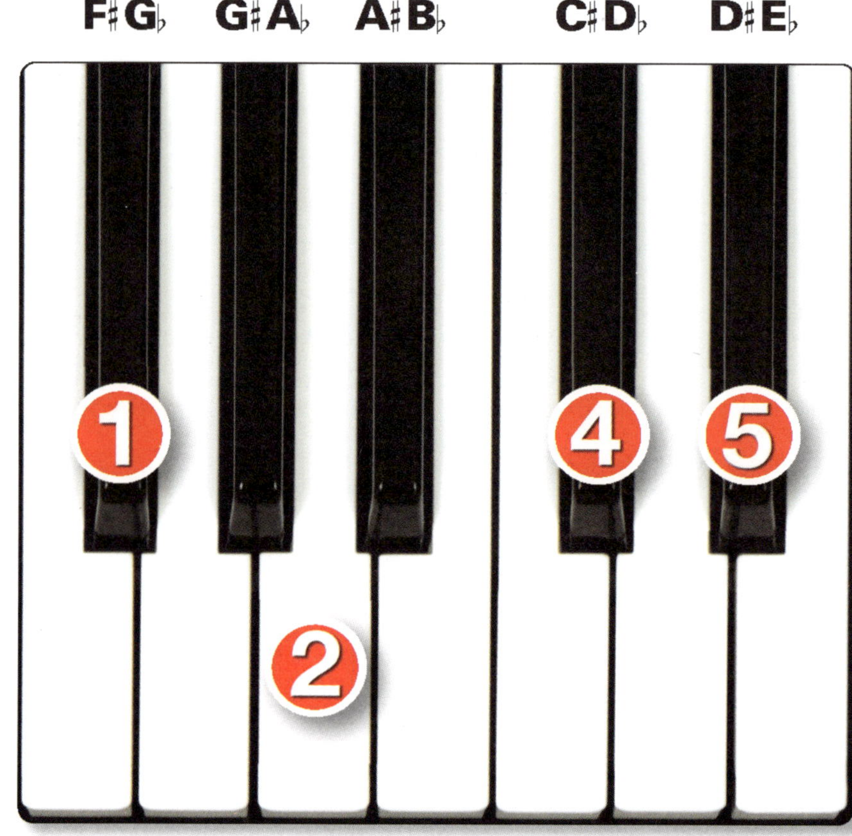

Chord Spelling

1st (F♯), ♭3rd (A), 5th (C♯), 6th (D♯)

Left hand suggestion: 1st (root note) and 5th

FREE ACCESS on smartphones including iPhone & Android

Using any free QR code app, scan and **HEAR** the chord

F♯/G♭maj7
Major 7th

Chord Spelling

1st (F♯), 3rd (A♯), 5th (C♯), 7th (F)

Left hand suggestion: 1st (root note) and 5th

FREE ACCESS on smartphones including iPhone & Android

Using any free QR code app, scan and **HEAR** the chord

Chord Spelling

1st (F♯), ♭3rd (A), 5th (C♯), ♭7th (E)

Left hand suggestion: 1st (root note) and 5th

FREE ACCESS on smartphones including iPhone & Android

Using any free QR code app, scan and **HEAR** the chord

F#/G♭7
Dominant 7th

Chord Spelling

1st (F#), 3rd (A#), 5th (C#), ♭7th (E)

Left hand suggestion: 1st (root note) and 5th

FREE ACCESS on smartphones including iPhone & Android

Using any free QR code app, scan and **HEAR** the chord

F♯/G♭°7
Diminished 7th

G♯A♭ A♯B♭ C♯D♭ D♯E♭

G A B C D E F

Chord Spelling

1st (F♯), ♭3rd (A), ♭5th (C), ♭♭7th (E♭)

Left hand suggestion: 1st (root note) and 5th

FREE ACCESS on smartphones including iPhone & Android

Using any free QR code app, scan and **HEAR** the chord

F♯/G♭maj9
Major 9th

Chord Spelling

1st (F♯), 3rd (A♯), 5th (C♯), 7th (E♯), 9th (G♯)

Left hand suggestion: 1st (root note) and 5th

FREE ACCESS on smartphones including iPhone & Android

Using any free QR code app, scan and **HEAR** the chord

G
Major

Chord Spelling

1st (G), 3rd (B), 5th (D)

Left hand suggestion: 1st (root note) and 5th

FREE ACCESS on smartphones including iPhone & Android

Using any free QR code app, scan and **HEAR** the chord

Gm
Minor

Chord Spelling

1st (G), ♭3rd (B♭), 5th (D)

Left hand suggestion: 1st (root note) and 5th

FREE ACCESS on smartphones including iPhone & Android

Using any free QR code app, scan and **HEAR** the chord

G+
Augmented Triad

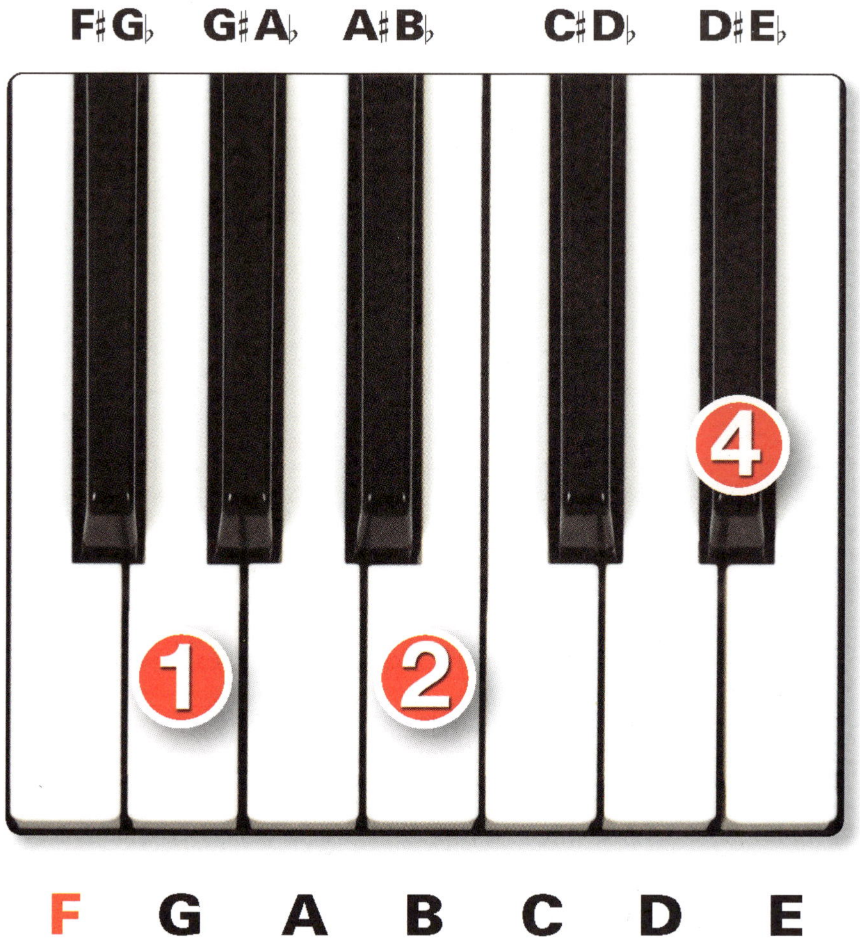

Chord Spelling

1st (G), 3rd (B), #5th (D#)

Left hand suggestion: 1st (root note) and 5th

G°
Diminished Triad

Chord Spelling

1st (G), ♭3rd (B♭), ♭5th (D♭)

Left hand suggestion: 1st (root note) and 5th

FREE ACCESS on smartphones including iPhone & Android

Using any free QR code app, scan and **HEAR** the chord

Gsus2
Suspended 2nd

Chord Spelling

1st (G), 2nd (A), 5th (D)

Left hand suggestion: 1st (root note) and 5th

FREE ACCESS on smartphones including iPhone & Android

Using any free QR code app, scan and **HEAR** the chord

Gsus4
Suspended 4th

Chord Spelling

1st (G), 4th (C), 5th (D)

Left hand suggestion: 1st (root note) and 5th

FREE ACCESS on smartphones including iPhone & Android

Using any free QR code app, scan and **HEAR** the chord

G5
5th (Power Chord)

Chord Spelling

1st (G), 5th (D)

Left hand suggestion: 1st (root note) and 5th

FREE ACCESS on smartphones including iPhone & Android

Using any free QR code app, scan and **HEAR** the chord

G6
Major 6th

Chord Spelling

1st (G), 3rd (B), 5th (D), 6th (E)

Left hand suggestion: 1st (root note) and 5th

Gm6
Minor 6th

Chord Spelling

1st (G), ♭3rd (B♭), 5th (D), 6th (E)

Left hand suggestion: 1st (root note) and 5th

FREE ACCESS on smartphones including iPhone & Android

Using any free QR code app, scan and **HEAR** the chord

Gmaj7
Major 7th

Chord Spelling

1st (G), 3rd (B), 5th (D), 7th (F#)

Left hand suggestion: 1st (root note) and 5th

FREE ACCESS on smartphones including iPhone & Android

Using any free QR code app, scan and **HEAR** the chord

Gm7
Minor 7th

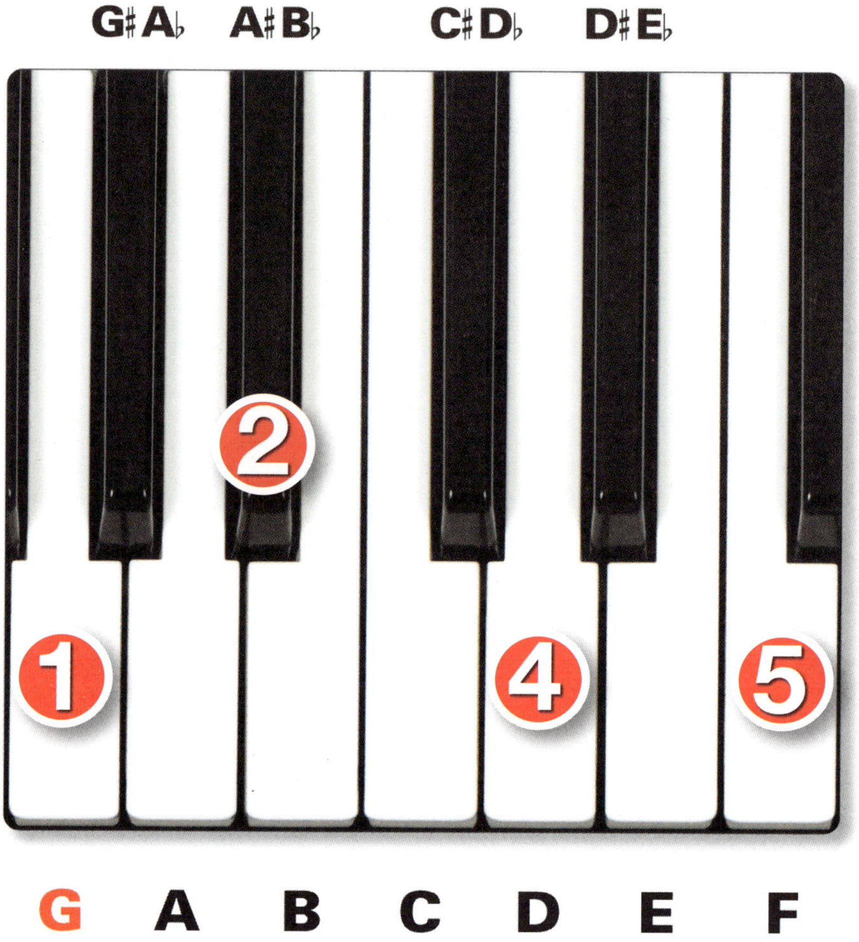

Chord Spelling

1st (G), ♭3rd (B♭), 5th (D), ♭7th (F)

Left hand suggestion: 1st (root note) and 5th

FREE ACCESS on smartphones including iPhone & Android

Using any free QR code app, scan and **HEAR** the chord

G7
Dominant 7th

Chord Spelling

1st (G), 3rd (B), 5th (D), ♭7th (F)

Left hand suggestion: 1st (root note) and 5th

FREE ACCESS on smartphones including iPhone & Android

Using any free QR code app, scan and **HEAR** the chord

G°7
Diminished 7th

Chord Spelling

1st (G), ♭3rd (B♭), ♭5th (D♭), ♭♭7th (F♭)

Left hand suggestion: 1st (root note) and 5th

FREE ACCESS on smartphones including iPhone & Android

Using any free QR code app, scan and **HEAR** the chord

Gmaj9
Major 9th

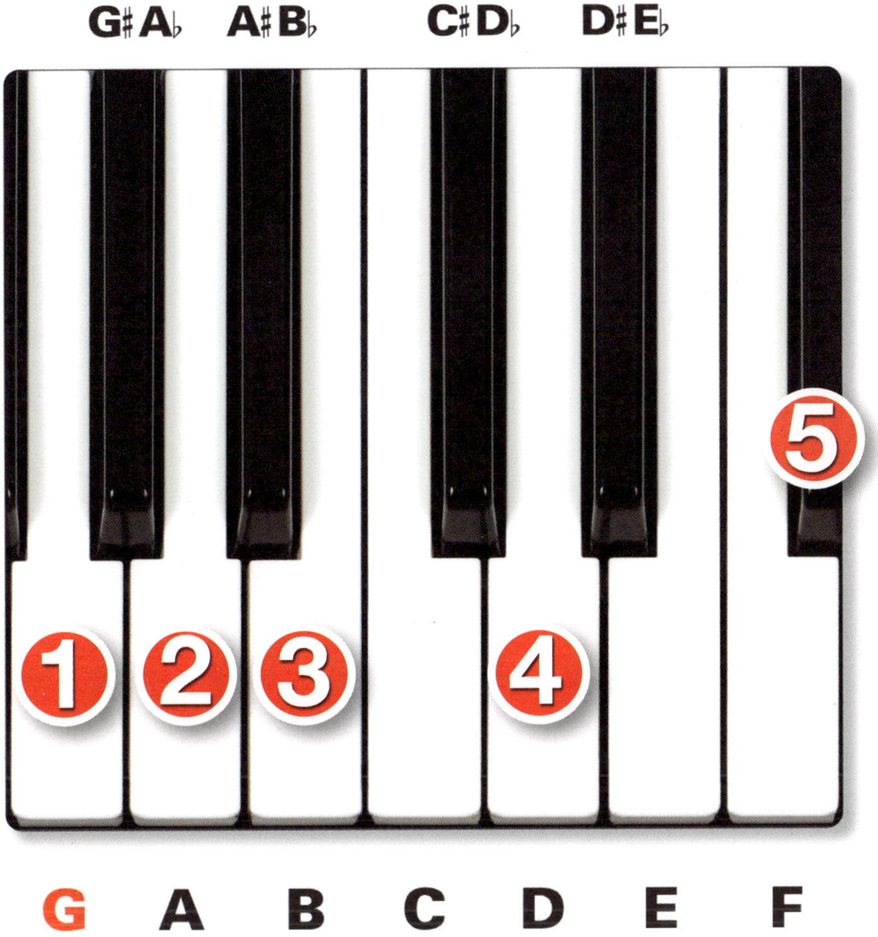

Chord Spelling

1st (G), 3rd (B), 5th (D), 7th (F#), 9th (A)

Left hand suggestion: 1st (root note) and 5th

FREE ACCESS on smartphones
including iPhone & Android

Using any free QR code app,
scan and **HEAR** the chord

G♯/A♭
Major

F♯G♭ G♯A♭ A♯B♭ C♯D♭ D♯E♭

F G A B C D E

Chord Spelling
1st (A♭), 3rd (C), 5th (E♭)

Left hand suggestion: 1st (root note) and 5th

G♯/A♭

FREE ACCESS on smartphones including iPhone & Android

Using any free QR code app, scan and **HEAR** the chord

G♯/A♭m
Minor

Chord Spelling

1st (A♭), ♭3rd (C♭), 5th (E♭)

Left hand suggestion: 1st (root note) and 5th

FREE ACCESS on smartphones including iPhone & Android

Using any free QR code app, scan and **HEAR** the chord

G♯/A♭

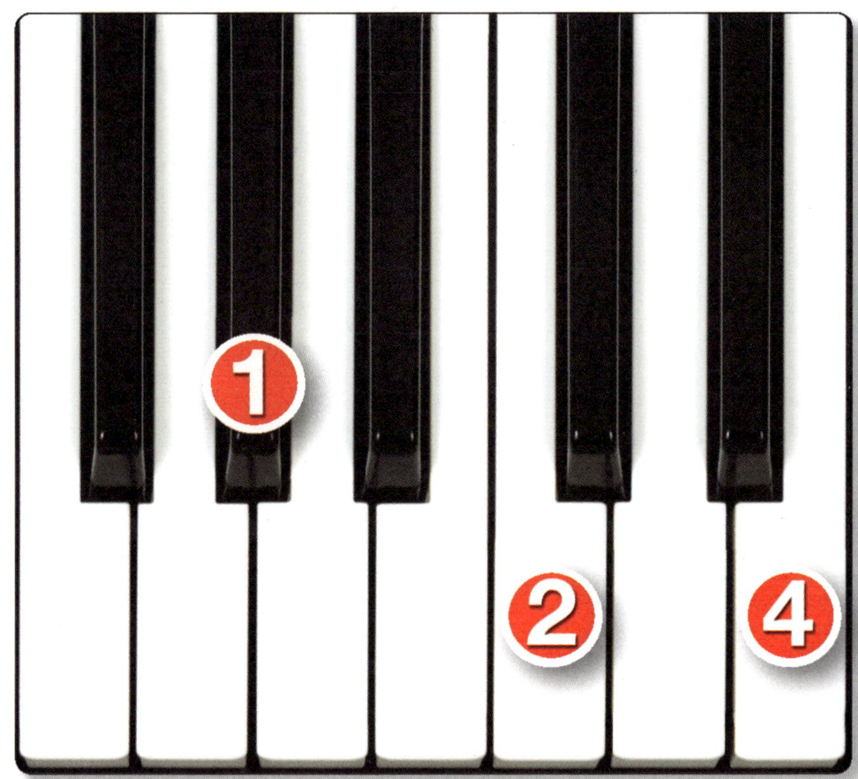

Chord Spelling
1st (A♭), 3rd (C), ♯5th (E)

Left hand suggestion: 1st (root note) and 5th

FREE ACCESS on smartphones including iPhone & Android

Using any free QR code app, scan and **HEAR** the chord

G♯/A♭°
Diminished Triad

Chord Spelling

1st (A♭), ♭3rd (C♭), ♭5th (E♭♭)

Left hand suggestion: 1st (root note) and 5th

FREE ACCESS on smartphones including iPhone & Android

Using any free QR code app, scan and **HEAR** the chord

G#/A♭sus2
Suspended 2nd

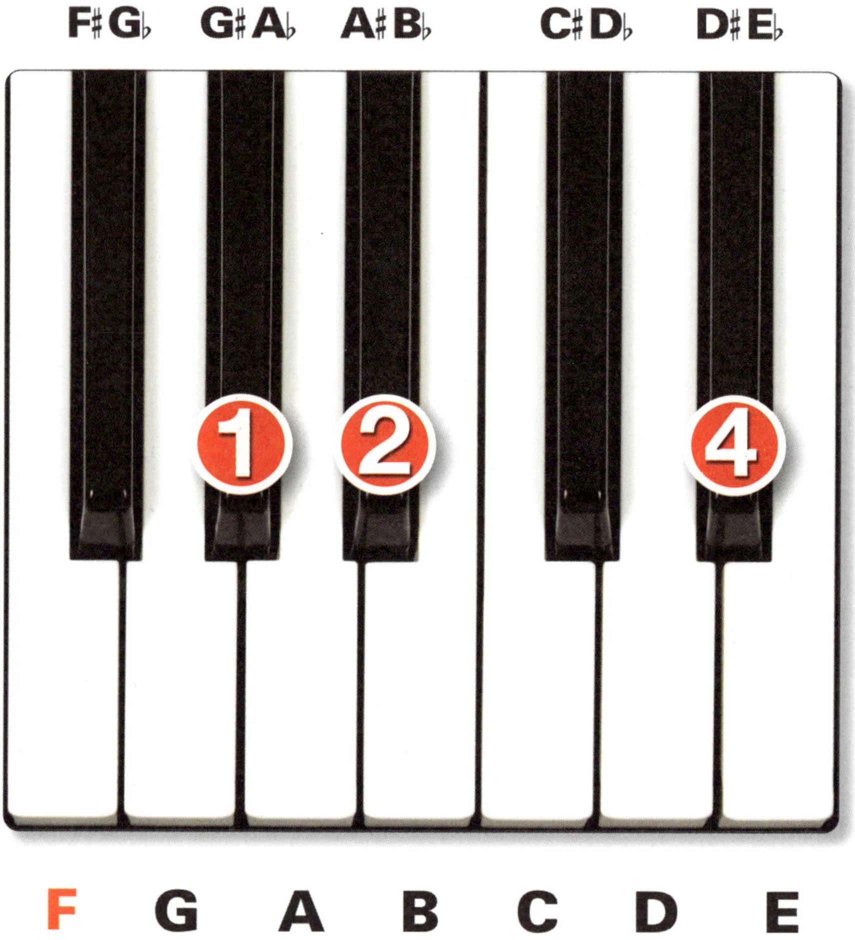

Chord Spelling

1st (A♭), 2nd (B♭), 5th (E♭)

Left hand suggestion: 1st (root note) and 5th

FREE ACCESS on smartphones including iPhone & Android

Using any free QR code app, scan and **HEAR** the chord

G♯/A♭sus4
Suspended 4th

Chord Spelling

1st (A♭), 4th (D♭), 5th (E♭)

Left hand suggestion: 1st (root note) and 5th

FREE ACCESS on smartphones including iPhone & Android

Using any free QR code app, scan and **HEAR** the chord

G♯/A♭

G♯/A♭5
5th (Power Chord)

Chord Spelling

1st (A♭), 5th (E♭)

Left hand suggestion: 1st (root note) and 5th

G♯/A♭

FREE ACCESS on smartphones including iPhone & Android

Using any free QR code app, scan and **HEAR** the chord

G♯/A♭6
Major 6th

Chord Spelling

1st (A♭), 3rd (C), 5th (E♭), 6th (F)

Left hand suggestion: 1st (root note) and 5th

FREE ACCESS on smartphones including iPhone & Android

Using any free QR code app, scan and **HEAR** the chord

G♯/A♭m6
Minor 6th

Chord Spelling

1st (A♭), ♭3rd (C♭), 5th (E♭), 6th (F)

Left hand suggestion: 1st (root note) and 5th

G♯/A♭

FREE ACCESS on smartphones including iPhone & Android

Using any free QR code app, scan and **HEAR** the chord

G♯/A♭maj7
Major 7th

Chord Spelling

1st (A♭), 3rd (C), 5th (E♭), 7th (G)

Left hand suggestion: 1st (root note) and 5th

FREE ACCESS on smartphones including iPhone & Android

Using any free QR code app, scan and **HEAR** the chord

G♯/A♭

G♯/A♭m7
Minor 7th

Chord Spelling

1st (A♭), ♭3rd (C♭), 5th (E♭), ♭7th (G♭)

Left hand suggestion: 1st (root note) and 5th

G♯/A♭7
Dominant 7th

Chord Spelling

1st (A♭), 3rd (C), 5th (E♭), ♭7th (G♭)

Left hand suggestion: 1st (root note) and 5th

FREE ACCESS on smartphones including iPhone & Android

Using any free QR code app, scan and **HEAR** the chord

G♯/A♭°7
Diminished 7th

Chord Spelling

1st (A♭), ♭3rd (C♭), ♭5th (E♭♭), ♭♭7th (G♭♭)

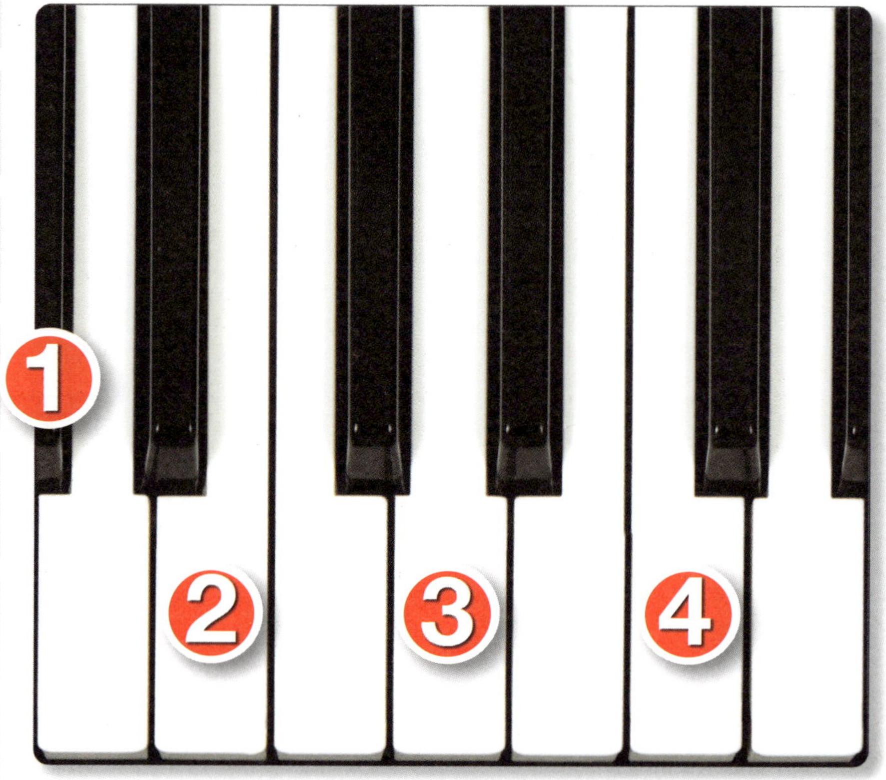

Left hand suggestion: 1st (root note) and 5th

G♯/A♭

FREE ACCESS on smartphones including iPhone & Android

Using any free QR code app, scan and **HEAR** the chord

G♯/A♭maj9
Major 9th

Chord Spelling

1st (A♭), 3rd (C), 5th (E♭), 7th (G), 9th (B♭)

Left hand suggestion: 1st (root note) and 5th

FREE ACCESS on smartphones including iPhone & Android

Using any free QR code app, scan and **HEAR** the chord

G♯/A♭

flametreemusic.com

The Flame Tree Music website complements our range of print books and offers easy access to chords and scales online, and on the move, through tablets, smartphones, and desktop computers.

1. The site offers access to chord diagrams and finger positions for both the guitar and the piano/keyboard, presenting a wide range of sound options to help develop good listening technique, and to assist you in identifying the chord and each note within it.

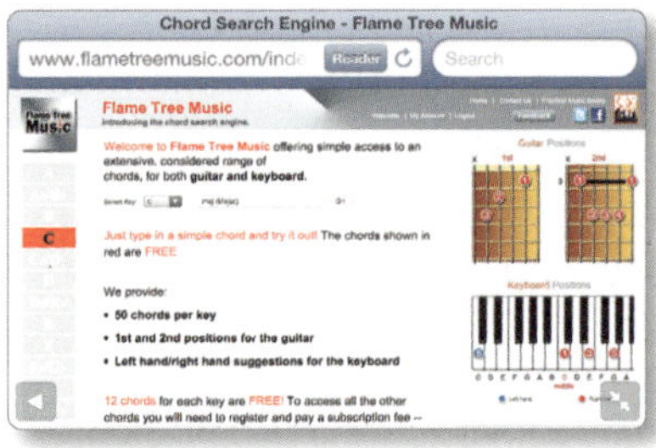

2. The site offers 12 **free** chords, those most commonly used in bands and songwriting.

3. A subscription is available if you'd like the full range of chords, **50** for **each key**.

4. Guitar chords are shown with **first** and **second positions on the fretboard**.

5. For the keyboard, you can **see** and **hear** each note in **left-** and **right-hand positions**.

6. Choose the key, then the chord name from the drop down menu. Note that the **red chords** are available **free**. Those in blue can be accessed with a subscription.

7. Once you've selected the chord, press **GO** and the details of the chord will be shown, with chord spellings, keyboard and guitar fingerings.

8. Sounds are provided in four easy-to-understand configurations.

9. flametreemusic.com also gives you access to **20 scales for each key**.

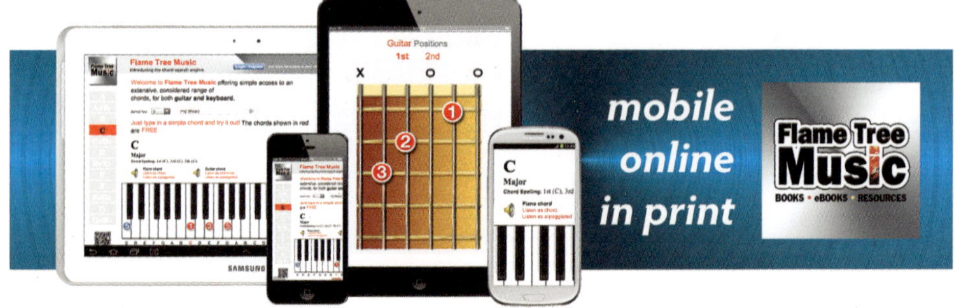